DISARMING THE PAST

DISARMING
the PAST

*How an Intimate Relationship
Can Heal Old Wounds*

JERRY M. LEWIS, M.D.

with

JOHN T. GOSSETT, PH.D.

ZEIG, TUCKER & CO., INC.
PHOENIX, ARIZONA

Library of Congress Cataloging-in-Publication Data

Lewis, Jerry M., 1924–
    Disarming the past : how an intimate relationship can heal old wounds /
Jerry M. Lewis with John T. Gossett.
        p.   cm.
    Includes bibliographical references and index.
    ISBN 1-891944-06-1
    1. Marriage—Psychological aspects.   2. Adult children of dysfunctional
families.   3. Psychotherapy.   4. Intimacy (Psychology)   I. Gossett, John
T., 1937–   II. Title.
HQ728.L7312   1999
158.2—dc21   98-33362
                                                                                CIP

Copyright © 1999 by Zeig, Tucker & Co., Inc.

Published by

ZEIG, TUCKER & CO., INC.
1928 East Highland, Suite F104-607
Phoenix, Arizona 85020

Manufactured in the United States of America

10   9   8   7   6   5   4   3   2   1

Acknowledgments

First, I owe my coauthor, John Gossett, my gratitude for insisting that the ideas in this book were too important either to discard or to leave to the often simplistic presentations of pop psychologists, and for helping me put them into words.

I also owe a large debt to those individuals, couples, and families who have either volunteered for our research projects or come to me for help. They have taught me much, and, as a consequence, will see here pieces of themselves, in disguised forms.

I wish to thank, as well, Mary Anne Leistra and Ann Supina for their patience and skillful typing of the various drafts.

Finally, my greatest debt is to my lover, best friend, and wife for 48 years, Pat. She is able to encourage a relationship with me in which she embraces both an intense connection and a generative solitude. There is nothing more to ask.
—*Jerry M. Lewis, M.D.*

I wish to thank Ann Supina and Mary Anne Leistra for translating my material into perfect copy quickly, and with unfailing good will.

Lisa and Mike Achee, Laura and Doug Austin, and Penny Riddle read various drafts. Their thoughtful reactions led to many changes.

Pam Riddle made scores of helpful suggestions as she read draft after draft. More important, though, she has helped me to understand the book's ideas in my heart.

—*John T. Gossett, Ph.D.*

Contents

Preface

Psychiatric training was, for me, the beginning of learning how to facilitate patients' stories (with as little direction as possible) and how to recognize the recurring patterns (usually of important relationships) embedded in those stories.

Marital and family research introduced me to the habit of making systematic observations of how stories come to be, of the conversational patterns that either encourage further exploration and richer narratives or shut them down.

Throughout this personal professional journey, I wrote about research findings, clinical insights, and new directions for the future. My writing was for other professionals and emphasized how complex we are as individuals, couples, and families.

Although this book is in my voice, it was my longtime friend and colleague, John Gossett, who pruned and augmented what I had to say, and shaped it into a form that would be more accessible to the general reader. It was truly a collaborative effort.

I am hopeful that others will find useful that which I have learned over the 40 years of my psychotherapeutic practice and John's and my shared research efforts. The topic—how some are able to work through childhood trauma in healing adult relationships—can make life something richer than the past. For those who do not construct a healing relationship, there is a strong likelihood that the painful past will be relived, often over and over again. And this underscores the necessity to think deeply about the central relationship patterns in life.

Jerry M. Lewis, M.D.

DISARMING THE PAST

The Idea of Marital Healing

What would happen if a new miracle drug were developed that could give you:

- better mental and physical health,
- deeper meaning in life,
- greater satisfaction in your everyday activities,
- and increased psychological health for your children?

Undoubtedly, there would be a great demand for the drug, the manufacturer would have trouble meeting the demand, the value of the company's stock would soar, and the developer of the drug would receive a Nobel Prize.

There is, of course, no such drug and little likelihood that one will be developed. The effects noted, however, can be brought about by something that most individuals can initiate on their own: *the construction of a good marriage.*

This book is about a particular feature of marriage—*the ability of a good relationship to heal participants who are suffering as a result of childhood abuse, neglect, rejection, or some other harmful life experience.* For many persons, marriage offers the single greatest possibility of undoing the past.

THE POSITIVE SIDE OF MARRIAGE

Although for years, researchers and teachers have been studying the negative aspects of marriage, such as marital dysfunction, marital conflict, and divorce, until recently, relatively little attention has been paid to the *positives.* What you may not know is that recent research shows that:

- The level of marital happiness is by far the strongest predictor of overall life satisfaction. (*Greater satisfaction in everyday activities*)

- On the average, married men and women live longer and suffer fewer illnesses than do single men and women. (*Better physical health*)

- Young men and women with histories of delinquency improve their chances of leading law-abiding, productive adult lives if they achieve a stable marriage. (*Better mental health*)

- Intravenous drug users who gave up drug use without any formal treatment often report that they did so because of a new and intense connection to another person. (*Better mental health*)

• Women who were abused as children are much less likely to abuse their own children if they have an emotionally supportive relationship with a partner. (*Increasing the psychological health of the children*)

• Women who experienced insecure attachments to their mothers during childhood are more apt to have insecure attachments with their own children, unless they marry men who have the capacity to attach securely to others. (*Increasing the psychological health of the children*)

• Men and women at greater risk than average for depression are not as likely to become depressed if they have an intimate, confiding relationship. (*Better mental health*)

• Women with serious behavior problems in childhood often continue to show a lack of self-control as adults and tend to exacerbate the situation by marrying passive men, whereas this problem might be avoided by selecting more assertive partners. (*Better mental health*)

• Confiding very personal thoughts to an accepting spouse leads to improved functioning of the immune system whereas episodes of marital conflict result in diminished immune system function. (*Better physical health*)

The evidence is growing that the quality of one's central relationship, most often a marriage, may have a profound impact on one's quality of life, overall life satisfaction, and emotional and physical health. Indeed, there is no more important adult decision in life than whom one chooses to marry. That decision will influence every moment of every day, for better or for worse, for you and your children. Although positive experiences with important friends, mentors, and lovers are helpful, there is no adult relationship with as much power to overcome and heal damaging childhood experiences as marriage.

Healing marriages can take many forms. The healing may mean learning to trust, or it may depend on other personal changes. To learn to stand alone, to speak out, to be more one's own person can be a healing process for some (developing a greater capacity for *separateness* or *autonomy*). For others, the healing means learning how to be close, how to recognize and share deep inner feelings and thoughts (developing a greater capacity for *connectedness* or *intimacy*). For still others, healing occurs when "old scripts" are given up, when personal imperfections are accepted, and when the differences between those we love and ourselves become a cause for celebration and not for criticism.

In all of these personality changes, as in the many others that may be observed, there is an increased capacity either for separateness, for connectedness, or for both. Healing leads in the direction of maturity and maturity involves the ability both to take good care of one's self independently and to truly connect—in a close, intimate way—with others.

chapter one

❧

A Little Bit of Theory

In order to place the idea of healing marriages in the context of current thinking about human development and maturation, it is necessary to describe some important beliefs that are held by many in the mental health disciplines. These beliefs can be illustrated with a clinical vignette.

Ellen, in her early 40s, chaired a department at a fine college. Her decision to enter individual psychotherapy was prompted by her anxiety symptoms and her inability to choose whether or not to marry a somewhat older, widowed colleague.

The oldest of four siblings, as a child, she had borne the brunt of her alcoholic father's physical abuse and her chronically depressed mother's unavailability. She said that she had tried to protect her younger sisters and to give them the emotional support that her mother had failed to provide.

Ellen thus became a very "good" little girl early in life. She never shared any of her deeper feelings, and her focus was almost entirely on academic success and her role as family care-taker.

Ellen's first close relationship was with Sue, her assigned roommate at college. Sue was outgoing, warm, and sensitive to the feelings of others. Over the four years that they roomed together, Ellen gradually disclosed to Sue something of her pain-ful childhood circumstances and her feelings about her parents. Although this was an unusual degree of self-disclosure for Ellen, she still did not reveal her deeper feelings of hurt and anger, nor did she develop any understanding that her reticence had been fostered by the abusiveness and unavailability of her par-ents. The relationship with her roommate, however, was crucial in that Sue made it safe for her to experiment with closeness for the first time.

In graduate school, Ellen quickly established herself as an out-standing student. Her doctoral dissertation was published and brought her both early recognition in her field and a tenured-track professorship offer from an excellent university.

She also experienced her first romance there. Bob, a fellow graduate student, was outgoing and likable. Their relationship gradually became sexual and Ellen discovered that, although she found pleasure in sex, she was unable to achieve orgasm. "It was the letting go that gave me trouble," she said. "Making out with Bob put me in touch with my incessant need to be in control of myself—and, I guess, of all important relationships."

The relationship ended when Ellen moved away to begin her teaching career. Looking back, she said, "It probably wasn't really being in love, but it was a very helpful relationship. It was as close as I had allowed myself to be to a man, and it was also my introduction to sex. I learned some things about relationships that are still important to me."

She also reported that although still primarily focused on her work, she became more accessible for friendships with other graduate students.

As a professor, Ellen again was outstanding. She was granted tenure in just a few years and was approached with job offers by other universities. These early years of academia brought Ellen a new form of relationship experience, that of mentoring students. As they came to know and trust her, they shared many personal feelings with her. Ellen found these relationships deeply satisfying, although she herself shared little of her deeper self with her students.

After ten years of productive academic life, Ellen accepted the chair of a department at a small, exclusive liberal arts college. It was here that she met Les, who also chaired a department there.

Les was 53 and had lost his wife five years earlier. He had two children, both of whom were in graduate school.

As they became close friends, Ellen and Les began to talk about personal matters and Les made such self-disclosure seem less dangerous. Their sexual relationship developed slowly and Ellen described Les as a considerate lover.

After several years of what both considered to be a deeply satisfying relationship, Les made it clear to Ellen that he wanted to marry her. In the context of his quiet but firm insistence, Ellen developed a more or less chronic level of low-grade anxiety. Her sleep became less consistent, and she called for her first appointment after experiencing a panic attack. She explained that the panic episode had occurred when she awoke from a short nap that followed a gratifying session of lovemaking.

DEVELOPMENT AND CHANGE ARE LIFELONG PROCESSES

In the 1950s, the prevalent view of human development was that an individual's basic personality is formed during early childhood. Only relatively minor modifications could be expected later, and, for the most part, only as the result of extensive psychotherapy or psychoanalysis. Whether this view focused on the inherited, "hard-wired" aspects of temperament or on the learned social patterns of childhood relationships, the consensus was that the average person with average everyday problems would demonstrate little change in personality during his or her lifetime.

Further, the idea of this relative unchangeability of the personality after childhood was often understood as being positive. That is, persons who did not appear to change very much were considered to have "stable" personalities; those who showed too much change over time were seen as unstable.

During more recent decades, there has been a shift in professional opinion to a growing emphasis on the *continuing development of the personality throughout adolescence and the adult years*. Currently, the most popular model of adult development focuses on alternating periods of stability and change. The periods during which changes occur are understood as "transitions," fueled mostly by age-specific developmental challenges. Thus, "young adulthood," for example, is seen as including separation emotionally from one's family of origin and the establishment of a primary emotional investment in a new love relationship; increased development of the capacity for emotional intimacy; and construction of an initial life dream or plan separate from the family of origin. Other adult periods have their own generally agreed-upon specific developmental challenges.

For the purpose of understanding healing marriages, it is important to emphasize that personality is now considered as continuing to develop throughout life.

To return to Ellen, it is obvious that her late adolescent and young adult periods demonstrate considerable changes in her personality—the growth of a new capacity for relationships and, in particular, the movement away from the narrow caretaking role she had learned as a child. Ellen has been able, gradually, to search for and accept a broader range of gratifications and to be more concerned with her own needs. Although she has not relinquished her reliance on her intellectual abilities, they now appear to be better balanced by her willingness to experiment with emotionally important relationships. Whether the focus is on her love affair with Les, her friendships, her mentoring of students, or the leadership role she plays in her department, the changes seem striking: Ellen has *changed during adulthood*; her ability to love is beginning to play a complementary role to her nearly lifelong capacity for sustained, hard work.

MORE THAN AUTONOMY IS NECESSARY

One of the goals of healthy human development is the capacity for connecting to others in ways that lead to a shared sense of closeness, which, in turn, gives special meaning to life. For most of this century, the Western perception of healthy human development emphasized the capacity for *separateness* and, in particular, for *autonomy*. The success of an individual's journey through life could be judged almost entirely by the extent to which he or she could separate from early family relationships and live autonomously. The hallmark of this view was success in competition—winning out over others.

It was never really hidden that this yardstick of successful development applied mostly to men. Until quite recently, women were expected to devote their lives to relationships with spouses, children, parents, and others. Men went out in the world to compete and conquer; women stayed home to nurture.

As these gender stereotypes began to change over the past 30 or so years, it became clear that *women's development, as well as that of men, should optimally lead to the capacities for both separateness and connectedness*. Men's development could no longer be seen as successful if the capacity for autonomy was not balanced by a comparable ability to enter into close relationships. The woman who relates intimately to others but has difficulty functioning autonomously also is seen as developmentally flawed.

> The most likely explanation of Ellen's early avoidance of close relationships relates to the combined effects of her abuse by her father and her mother's emotional unavailability and failure to protect her. Thus, early in life, she came to the *unconscious conclusion* that by getting close to another, one runs the risk of either assault or abandonment. These fears can be powerful reasons to avoid closeness. Ellen's only childhood experiences of safe, although limited, closeness involved successful achievement through hard work and compliance (do the "right" thing well, and don't let others know what you really feel) and caretaking (strive to be in control of relationships by always taking care of others).
>
> At college, Ellen showed her ability to function autonomously. Her capacity for separateness was strong and well practiced. She avoided close relationships, however, and if she were to mature, she had to risk facing her underlying fears. Her capacity for *connectedness* was inhibited by unconscious fears from childhood. She could work, but not love. Closeness to others was not possible. Her injury needed healing.

GROWTH AND MATURATION REQUIRE AN AFFIRMING OTHER

There are two basic ideas as to how individual maturation occurs across the life span. One emphasizes the role of factors *inside the individual,* without giving much attention to the influence of other persons or events. It is inherited traits or early personality characteristics that are seen as important influences on the individual's approaches to adult developmental challenges.

The interpersonal perspective adds the idea that it is the nature of one's important relationships that is crucial to growth and maturation. One will find it extremely difficult to attain maturity without the assistance of influential "teachers"—parents, siblings, other relatives, close friends, actual teachers, mentors, romantic partners.

Most of those who emphasize that relationships promote maturation do not discount the importance of individual characteristics. Rather, they emphasize three interacting groups of factors: the individual's characteristics, the characteristics of the important other, and the nature of the relationship that is constructed by the two partners. In this view, the nature of the relationship cannot be predicted on the basis of the two partners' individual personalities; rather, the relationship is characterized by unpredictable, "emergent" features that are crucial for maturation.

> Ellen's maturation, shown in her increased capacity for entering intimate relationships, can be understood as a consequence of a series of relationship experiences. She first learned to talk a bit about the unfortunate circumstances of her childhood with Sue, her college roommate. But without more complete information, we cannot know how much this reflected her

being assigned to a sensitive, warm, and outgoing roommate; how much it resulted from Ellen's leaving home and finding the hidden inner strengths to take a chance and begin relating more openly to a peer; or how much it came out of magic moments that evoked a mutual sharing of painful experiences.

Ellen's romantic involvement with Bob can also be understood as an early "experiment" with closeness and intimacy. Once again, it appears that the other person took the lead in establishing the relationship. He was able to make it safe for Ellen to experiment with physical intimacy. It is also important to recognize that because Bob was respectful and trustworthy, Ellen was not hurt in this relationship. *She felt neither abused nor abandoned;* their involvement ended naturally when she finished graduate school. Her unconscious childhood fears were powerfully contradicted by her relationships with both Sue and Bob.

During these years, Ellen developed friendships with several other students, and these, too, added to her experiences of closeness. Later, as a young professor, Ellen became a sought-after mentor, and this also increased her interest in closeness and intimacy.

It is with Les, however, that Ellen faces the challenge of committing herself to a permanent relationship. In particular, Les's capacity for the sensitive exploration of very personal matters—both his and Ellen's—contains the seeds of both a rewarding intimacy and the dangerous possibility of deep hurt. *Intimacy has at its core vulnerability*, and the anxiety that brought Ellen to therapy sprang from this unconscious conflict between the wish for intimacy and the fear of being hurt.

How Do We Change Each Other?

It is clear that we have much to learn in this area. However, there are several theories that can help us begin to understand.

Both General and Specific Healing Processes Are At Work

A relationship with an important other may infuse one's entire emotional environment with attitudes and behaviors that encourage growth.

Recent research suggests that an important growth-enhancing relationship feature is the *process of confiding*—the ability of two persons to share inner feelings and thoughts. What is it that stimulates the process? I propose that it is the combination of *empathy, warmth, and genuineness.* If one partner is *sensitive to the feelings* of the other and reacts in an *honest* and *affectionate way,* he or she provides conditions that may lead to safe confiding and assure that the results will be helpful.

A second line of thought involves each partner's providing a specific attitude, behavior, or capability that the other person lacks or needs. An example is the finding that women with severe behavior problems who marry passive men persist in their poor self-control, whereas similar women who marry more assertive men do not have continuing behavior-control problems. These latter husbands provide some behavioral limits that are missing in the women—their assertiveness is a specific part of the emotional climate that encourages maturation for their wives.

IS HEALING ALWAYS RECIPROCAL?

An interesting question regarding the interpersonal approach to individual maturation involves the idea of reciprocity. Does individual maturation always occur in both partners, or are couples observed in which only one partner appears to have matured as a result of the relationship?

In the initial interviews with Ellen, one could only guess at the mechanisms by which her relationships with Sue, Bob, mentored students, and, most important, Les had had positive impacts on her maturation. Of great importance, however, is the fact that she did not feel injured in any of these relationships. As a result, she risked increasing openness in each new relationship without feeling either abused or abandoned.

With Les, in particular, Ellen was able to experience the emotional climate that can promote maturation. His empathy, warmth, and genuineness assisted in establishing a safe place for the growth of her trust and confiding. Her unconscious fears of being abused or abandoned gradually receded.

Without talking to Les, it is impossible to ascertain what he received from the relationship, but it seems unlikely (based on Ellen's description of Les) that he experienced personal growth and change as profound as hers.

THERE ARE ALWAYS OTHERS
IN THE ROOM

Those in the mental health disciplines generally agree that childhood relationships are incorporated into a child's developing personality and so influence all relationships throughout life. Whether one calls them "internal images of early relationships," "inner working models," "cognitive schemata," or "assumptive sets," they all emphasize one principle: the impact of the past on the present. One is never truly alone with an important other because both partners bring into the relationship unconscious hopes, fears, and expectations developed during their early formative years.

This strong tendency to recreate early relationship patterns may work in either positive or negative ways. The little girl who was treated as very special by her parents may search for, and find, a life partner who needs to have a spouse he experiences as extraordinary, and this can benefit both partners. The little boy who was physically abused by his mother and, as an adult, enters a series of relationships with abusive women, is a not uncommon example of the negative consequences of this tendency.

There is much to suggest that internalized relationship patterns from childhood are not easy to change. It takes an intense emotional relationship, usually one of many months or years in duration, to bring change about. Although for some, *psychotherapy* is the vehicle for accomplishing these changes, *marriage* is the most common human connection in which unhealthy, destructive, or self-defeating early relationship patterns are worked through and extinguished.

> The anxiety that brought Ellen to therapy can be understood as arising from the conflict between her conscious wish to commit to a close and intimate relationship with Les and the arousal of her unconscious fears of abuse and abandonment. She had been without significant anxiety until Les pressed her for a commitment. After only a few interviews, it seemed clear that Ellen needed to face her hidden fears if she were going to continue her search for closeness and intimacy at this time in her life.

This brief synopsis of the first several interviews with Ellen provides an example of important principles of the maturation of the human personality and the crucial roles that relationships with others play in this growth.

UNANSWERED QUESTIONS

We accept that healing occurs, but there are many questions yet to be answered. Most important, it is not fully known why some persons with traumatic childhoods find healing relationships that transform their lives, whereas others do not. Some remain isolated and incapable of closeness and intimacy. Others enter into adult relationships that involve new experiences of abuse or abandonment that echo and reinforce the effects of the childhood traumas. For the fortunate, however, the consequences of

the harmful past are worked through in an adult love relationship. Luck, of course, may have something to do with it. It was
lucky for Ellen that Les, as a colleague, was available to her.
However, luck can only be a piece of the puzzle. Ellen had to
have the capacity to enter the relationship and to "use" it in a
positive way—to allow it to become a healing process.

To aid our understanding of relationships that heal, we need
to take a look at a most slippery concept, *the unconscious.*

THE UNCONSCIOUS

Paula, a long-term psychotherapy patient who had mastered
the art of identifying the unconscious wishes, fears, conflicts, and
motives that troubled her, "played therapist" with her lover in
the midst of an intense argument, telling him:

*"You're not really mad at me, Dave—you're still just furious
at your dad for being so mean to you."*

"Well, Dave just *exploded,*" she reported with great surprise.
"He stuck his face right into mine and *yelled* as loudly as he
could, 'I'm mad at *you,* not my dad!' Then he bolted out of the
house, slamming the door so hard that the walls shook."

Without trying to reconstruct the multiple sources of Dave's
anger, it is safe to say that anger often "covers up" other important feelings. Lurking behind angry feelings may be fears or
hurts *of which we are unaware.*

Dave no doubt was correct in maintaining that he *was* angry at Paula—but she also was right in assuming that a hidden, unspoken fear or hurt probably was heaping fuel on the fires of his rage. The rationale for the assumption is that *the anger was so disproportionate to the provocation.* Paula had made a minor change in their plans for the day without informing him—a change that ordinarily would have stimulated a minor response (or no response at all) from good-natured Dave.

What was different about this exchange was that Paula was due to move out-of-state to begin a new position, and Dave had decided to stay behind rather than give up his job.

Often abused, and eventually abandoned, by his father, Dave was hypersensitive to being left by someone he loved and needed. So, in her way, Paula was on target in her confrontation. Dave's unconscious rage toward his father most likely was reignited by his fear of losing Paula as well. But this connection was outside of Dave's awareness; it was *unconscious.*

This brings us to the second major point about unconscious fears and motivations: nobody wants to hear about them.

Novice psychotherapists, well trained to *detect contradictions or discrepancies* in their patients' words and actions (which often signal the operation of unconscious fears and motives), frequently blurt out their newly found discoveries to their patients, much as Paula did with Dave.

"Explosion" is often the patient's response, just as it was Dave's.

Experienced therapists learn to proffer these observations

very slowly and tentatively, never during an argument, and only after seeing the connections that are invisible to the patient.

A feeling of anger at being misunderstood and misinterpreted naturally follows any unsolicited confrontation regarding our motives. We *know* (consciously) why we do what we do. Dave knew that he was furious at Paula, and it magnified his anger to be told by her that his "real" motives lay elsewhere, and that she could read his behavior better than he could.

There is a saying among psychotherapists: "All behavior patterns are overdetermined." Translation: All behavior patterns have several (or many) causes, all operating at once; and never just one cause (which explains how both Dave and Paula could be correct).

The power of the dynamic unconscious—forces within us, of which we are unaware, that influence our thoughts, feelings, and actions—is one of the great legacies of Sigmund Freud's theories of personality. Coming to know your own "unconscious" involves learning how to see contradictions, discrepancies, and inconsistencies in your reactions that hint at hidden meanings. This is most effectively accomplished in insight-oriented psychotherapy or psychoanalysis, but both are extremely time consuming, expensive, and very hard work for both the patient and the therapist.

Supportive psychotherapy, like friendship, mentoring, and love, seeks to help through the relationship itself (without necessarily focusing on unconscious factors). This more popular approach is briefer and less expensive than the other therapies, and so is more available to more people.

Even more commonly, though, our early fears and conflicts are gradually worked through—healed—by close, enduring friendships; by good mentoring from wise and compassionate teachers; and, especially, by long-term committed love.

Why do we have "unconscious" memories? Why don't we just remember everything that comes into our brains, like a computer remembers everything in its memory storage? For our purposes, perhaps the most important reason is that we *pass judgment on ourselves (and others)* whereas computers do not.

It is in response to these self-evaluations that we find it necessary to defend ourselves against the conscious awareness of many deep, inner memories and feelings in order to keep our self-image positive and avoid crippling anxiety, guilt, and shame. Similarly, we have to defend ourselves against our real reasons for many of our daily actions in order to maintain our self-esteem. And, in addition, we have to "forget" much of what we know about our parents' mistakes—*especially* if they were abusive or neglectful—if we are to maintain a "positive" image of them. A small child, totally dependent on parents for love, nurturance, protection, and *life itself,* cannot afford to view a bad parent as an enemy to be avoided.

As a result of this tendency to defend ourselves against unpleasant memories or motives, we can see the "true personality" of another more clearly than we can see our own.

A husband tells the couples therapist, "My wife is *disorganized.*"

"I am not," she replies, "I'm *spontaneous*. You, on the other hand, are *controlling*."

"No, you're wrong. I am *planful*, but never controlling."

As with Dave and Paula, both spouses *are correct*. Each sees his or her own good qualities clearly while being genuinely blind to any negative characteristics.

In couples therapy, if this couple is like most, they will not become aware of their unconscious feelings, actions, and motives by suddenly "remembering" or "seeing" them, but rather by learning to trust the observations and confrontations of a respected therapist, and eventually those of the newly respected spouse.

chapter two

———————— ⚭ ————————

The Dynamics of the Healing Marriage

We look to several sources to help us understand what puts the "healing" in healing marriages. Some of our data are drawn from longitudinal studies of persons at high risk for psychiatric disorders, such as depression and alcoholism. In these studies, *not* developing the disorder is associated with being in an emotionally intense, confiding relationship, usually a marriage. Healing marriages are also demonstrated by research volunteer couples who are functioning well both as couples and as individuals, but present a history of disturbed childhoods and the resulting traumas that have been overcome through the marital relationship. Another source of information is marital therapy, in which the therapist helps by beginning a process of healing that either had never taken place or was stalled somewhere along the way.

The search for healing is important, but it is only one part of the story. The other part is the strong tendency to repeat abusive, neglectful relationships from childhood with one's adult partner. This tendency to repeat—or "transference," as it is called by mental health professionals—is also an unconscious process. Although few people would deliberately search for an abusive adult partner, many actually end up with marriages that mirror their harmful childhood relationships. For others, the roles are switched; rather than being the abused adult partner, they become the abuser. Mental health professionals call this reversal "identification with the aggressor" because the child had taken into his or her personality the characteristics of the abusing or neglectful adult.

It is, then, more to the point to frame the question of the dynamics of healing marriages in terms of the unconscious civil war going on within many persons who experienced harmful childhoods, a war between the tendency to repeat and the search for healing.

QUESTIONS ABOUT HEALING MARRIAGES

Can you actually study the process of healing as it is occurring?

The answer to this question is, "Not yet." We have come to understand healing marriages after the process of healing has been accomplished. We look at the relationship after it has been formed, and study its essential characteristics. Our conclusion is that forming a certain type of relationship has resulted in healing for one or both partners, or that the healing process has triumphed over the repeating process.

Is there only one kind of healing marriage?

The answer is a clear "No." Although we do not know exactly how many types of healing marriages there are, we do know that the effects can range from subtle to dramatic. Healing marriages may lead to changes in personality characteristics, such as less rigidity, greater openness, clearer self-definitions, and increased assertiveness in either one or both spouses.

Healing marriages may prevent the development of psychiatric syndromes or improve the response to treatment of existing emotional disorders. This issue is controversial for some, partly owing to ignorance of the natural course of many psychiatric disorders. A large group of studies suggests that among patients with psychiatric disturbances, at least half either get over the disorder in time or learn to manage it without significant additional disability. These processes of recovery and improvement often take years, but longitudinal studies demonstrate that we have been far too pessimistic about the outcome of such disorders—in large part because those who do not recover remain highly visible whereas those who do blend into the general population. Further, and most relevant here, these studies emphasize that recovery or improvement is often associated with a new and intense relationship.

Some relationships appear to heal by providing one or both partners with perhaps one or two of the ingredients missing from their personalities, whereas others result in a much more substantial overhaul of the personality of one or both partners. Introverts can become more outgoing; poorly controlled, impulsive persons can develop more self-control; and those with very controlling personalities can learn to share.

Should I deliberately search for a healing marriage?

One of the ironies of healing marriages is that you are unlikely to find one by searching for it. Although you may be unconsciously drawn to someone with whom you will either repeat or repair an earlier relationship, the conscious search for healing usually fails. Why is this so? The most likely underlying reason is that the earlier destructive relationship is stored in nonverbal sections of the developing brain, and it thus takes an intense and sustained emotional arousal to reawaken those stored memories.

Persons who enter into adult relationships with the conscious need either to heal or to be healed are almost always disappointed. "I knew he was depressed (alcoholic, shy) and I thought I could help him." "She was so strong and forceful that I believed she could help me." These are the type of statements commonly inspired by failed relationships.

Some persons, however, are able to identify what to watch out for and can use this information to avoid entering into relationships with adults who have important characteristics similar to those displayed by harmful adults from their childhoods. In this way, they can avoid repeating the past. Even here, however, your mind can play tricks on you. You may see a potential adult partner as strong, for example, only to discover that he or she is distant, remote, and emotionally unavailable. Thus, although we may be able to avoid relationships that repeat the past, it is unlikely that we can consciously select a partner with whom healing will occur.

How long does it take for a marriage to heal?

Evidence suggests that the healing process usually takes at least several years. One is rarely healed by relatively brief encounters, because healing necessitates hundreds or thousands of interchanges between partners. If, for example, you learned in childhood that seeking closeness often leads to being hurt, you will likely need many experiences of closeness with your adult partner in which you are not hurt (rejected, abandoned, criticized, judged) before your inner fear of closeness is extinguished. Each repetition of the past must be countered by many more experiences in which the past is not repeated. Since no partner can always be sensitive to your needs and fears, the healing process is one of experimentation, improvement, failure, retreat, further experimentation, more improvement, and on and on.

Thus, healing involves pain, the pain of disappointment in the partner's response. It also requires hope, the willingness to try again and again. Some persons will seize on the partner's inevitable "misses" and give up hope. Others will focus on those occasions when the past is not repeated and continue to experiment. Why do some give up and others persist? I believe that gratitude and remorse are involved. Some of us are better able than others to express thankfulness and to apologize. That remorse and gratitude are crucial to all important relationships must be appreciated if the healing process is to succeed.

Can I expect a healing relationship with a spouse to be enough?

Although healing relationships provide the most common pathway to emotional growth and maturity, there is much to be gained from other relationships, including those with good friends, mentors, and siblings. In a similar vein, group processes can be very helpful. Active participation in Sunday school classes, an executive breakfast group, a writing workshop, or any other cohesive small group in which self-disclosure takes place can of great help.

Formal psychotherapy—individual, group, or marital/family—can play a decisive role for many. The appropriate use of prescribed psychotropic medicines can, by reducing crippling symptoms, such as anxiety or depression, make self-exploration, new learning, and emotional maturation more likely. In fact, it is self-defeating not to use the advances of the neurosciences to aid in the search for emotional maturity.

The key point is that there are multiple roads to wellness, and, although the importance of healing relationships is emphasized here, you should use as many of these roads as you can to overcome the lingering effects of harmful childhood relationships.

GENERAL PRINCIPLES OF HEALING MARRIAGES

• *Healing marriages involve taking into one's self characteristics of important others.*

Throughout life, even in infancy, we borrow some characteristics of important others. This central mechanism of emotional maturation is at the heart of the theory of personality development endorsed by many mental health professionals. Although these "internalizations" and "identifications" are silent processes that take place without our knowledge, they may change who we are, often in dramatic ways. Indeed, our basic sense of self can be changed through exchanges with an important other, in which we learn to be more like a deeply admired other or less like those whom we do not admire.

Early in our marriage, my wife confronted me with the fact that I was beginning to talk like my mentor. I was entirely unaware that I was using more and more of his inflections and pronunciations until she pointed it out. On another occasion, I realized, during a professional talk, that I had just said something in a way that was much like that of a revered senior colleague and unlike my usual delivery. After the talk, a close friend said that he had also noticed it, and he handed me a piece of paper on which he had written my colleague's name. These are but small examples of taking into one's self desirable attributes of important others. Of greater importance is the exchange of personality characteristics with one's spouse—the type of exchange that I believe is common in a shared life.

* *Healing most often involves a greater capacity either for connectedness (closeness, commitment, and intimacy) or for separateness (independence, autonomy, and solitude).*
  This insight, I believe, is a core feature of the healing process and the hallmark of the mature person. We learn to overcome fears of closeness or separateness, and move to a position in which we can more comfortably relate closely to an important other and take better care of ourselves.

  In my clinical practice of couples therapy, fears of closeness appear to be far more common than are fears of separateness. In reality, however, these fears are closely related. Most of those whom I see outwardly seem to be incapable of relating closely to an important other. Almost always this can be traced to one of two childhood circumstances: enduring an abusive, rejecting, or other harmful relationship with a parent, or growing up in a family that did not model closeness. But when one examines the fear of closeness, one finds that beneath it is the fear of separateness! It is because we fear abandonment, rejection, or not being needed (all forms of being alone) that we avoid closeness.

  Healing processes are thus understood to lead to a greater capacity for connecting closely to others, to a greater capacity for being alone, and, most often, to greater capacities for both.

• *Healing marriages are effective regulatory mechanisms.*
A major change in our understanding of marriage is that we
now recognize that, at its best, it serves to regulate the
spouses' feelings and behaviors. In other words, the unwrit-
ten rules of the relationship act as auxiliary psychological
support and control mechanisms for the participants. Most
of our professional attention in this regard has focused on
self-esteem regulation. A relationship should assist both partners in their individual efforts to maintain a positive level of
self-esteem, and it should help them to recover from inevitable disappointments and failures without suffering a longlasting negative impact. It should also help regulate excesses
of self-esteem, when a partner's positive feelings about himself or herself are beginning to shade into unrealistic gran-
diosity.

A healing marriage also assists in the regulation of other
aspects of individual functioning. It can help the individual
better regulate his or her impulses and feelings. And it also
can aid in clarifying one's basic sense of self. Although much
of this basic sense of self is formed early in childhood, it now
appears that throughout our lives, we are continually redefining our basic values and what we think and feel. A well-
functioning relationship assists both partners in these
ongoing processes of personal assessment, change, new stability, reassessment, further change, and so on.

Perhaps the most exciting research into the regulatory
function of relationships involves our physical functioning.

The evidence is mounting that specific features of the central relationship—such as the process of *confiding*—improve blood-pressure regulation and immune-system functioning. Other relationship features, such as *conflict*, impair those important physical functions.

Thus, it would seem that one way in which marriages can heal is through their regulatory functions. Persons change when they adopt new rules (usually not articulated), and in healing marriages, these rules enhance individual psychological functioning by encouraging some behaviors and discouraging others.

• *Healing marriages involve a balance of empathy (plus warmth and genuineness) and clarification–confrontation.* Three of the essential processes of effective psychotherapy also characterize communication in well-functioning marriages. Spouses in such marriages often talk with each other as if each were the other's therapist. In fact, a woman at a couples therapy session commented that one didn't really need a professional therapist if one's spouse had become the therapist.

Empathy, warmth, and genuineness are the core characteristics of effective psychotherapists. *Empathy* is the ability to be aware of what another person is feeling and to let that person know that you understand. It is centrally concerned with feelings, and we have long underestimated the role of feelings in how well or badly life turns out. Daniel Goleman, who pulled together much of the research about feelings, coined the term "emotional intelligence." The key to emotional intelligence is sensitivity to feelings—both one's own feelings and those of important others. Whether one studies marriages, infant–parent attachment, or psychotherapies, empathy proves to be a crucial factor in their success.

My 30 years of experience in teaching empathy to beginning psychotherapists have proved to me that empathy can be learned, and that a person's empathic ability can be improved.

How often are spouses really empathic with each other? I know that I am occasionally with my wife, but it is not, I'm afraid, the rule. I asked a good friend, an accomplished therapist, how often he was empathic with his spouse. He smiled and shook his head. I then asked him if he thought he was empathic 30 percent of the time. He laughed and said, "Jerry, if I were empathic that often, she wouldn't let me out of her sight!"

I used 30 percent for a reason. Although I can find no studies of the rate of empathy in marriage or psychotherapy, I did come across such a study of maternal empathic sensitivity with infants. The most sensitive mothers studied (by observing videotapes of infant–mother interactions) were empathic with their infants only 30 percent of the time. This suggests that a 30 percent rate is all that is necessary for a secure attachment. If something of the same order is present in a marriage, the marriage may be in very good shape.

Warmth and genuineness are the hallmarks of an inter-

ested other. These attributes in an important other increase the likelihood that one will learn more about one's
self and that the conversation will lead to greater exploration. Being genuine does not mean just saying anything
that comes to mind or doing whatever one wishes. Rather,
it is being authentic, trustworthy, without pretense or de-
ception.

Clarification occurs when one partner assists the other
to explore more thoroughly what the other is thinking or
feeling. Although empathic responses often lead to deeper
exploration and new insights, clarification is accomplished
by encouraging the other to put his or her thoughts into
words even though they may not be complete, may be
uncertain, or may contain conflicting themes. Questions
are helpful, particularly those that *open up topics* rather
than *narrow the focus.* "Playing back" what one has heard
in the form of brief summaries can be very helpful in that
this encourages the other to elaborate further on his or
her initial thoughts. Thus, as empathy is the major high-
way to feeling connected to an important other, clarification helps us understand how we are different (or
separate) from important others.

Confrontation usually provokes images of angry interactions. But that is not the type of confrontation to which
I am referring here. There are times in all relationships
when one partner receives contradictory messages from
the other. It may mean saying that everything is fine, but

with a gloomy facial expression. It may mean saying something that contradicts what one has said previously. It may mean doing something dangerous, apparently without realizing the danger. In all of these situations, there is an element of denial. Either consciously, or, more often, unconsciously, the person is behaving in a contradictory manner, and an important other who wishes to be helpful needs to say something. The contradiction needs to be addressed. This is what I mean by confrontation—the pointing out of a contradiction.

It is *how* one addresses the contradiction that is important. To do so with anger or some other negative emotion usually obviates the hoped-for helpful outcome. Contradictions must be confronted tactfully and, whenever possible, in a neutral or caring way. Confrontation is a way we help each other to face the inevitable contradictions in our lives and to come to know ourselves better. In this way, it helps us to develop a clearer sense of who we are.

SPECIFIC DYNAMICS OF HEALING RELATIONSHIPS

What I am going to describe is so crucial to all three "good" relationships (marriage, parent–infant, and therapist–patient) that I am convinced that it is at the heart of what makes for healing.

Research has shown that the dynamics are the same in the

three very different types of relationships—if the relationship is working well. Surely, if the same dynamics are at the core of such different kinds of relationship, they must be of unusual importance in the process of healing.

There are three parts to these dynamics:

1. The ability to come together, connect, and feel very close on some occasions.

2. The ability to remain separate (or to be alone) while together.

3. The ability to repair any hurt or damage following those occasions on which one partner wants to connect and the other fails to do so.

Connecting with an important other is accomplished by understanding, accepting, and respecting his or her subjective reality. It means really listening, focusing often on the other's feelings, helping the other to explore what is on his or her mind (rather than what is on your mind), suspending judgment, and avoiding attempts to suggest solutions (unless they are clearly requested). The partner describing an inner or outer experience will perceive the interest of the other and often will come to feel deeply understood. It is when two persons reach this level of shared understanding that there is apt to be a sense of real connection—even, at times, a sense of oneness.

Such experiences of connection need not occur often to be

of great significance. For some couples, there may be several minutes of connecting each day. But perhaps more commonly, such connecting happens less frequently. And many couples spend a lifetime together and never connect. Some don't even miss it—they are satisfied with distant relationships.

Couples who come for therapy most often are openly conflicted around the issue of connecting. One partner wants more connecting and the other does not. My task is to assist them to learn to connect.

The second part is the ability to be alone with an important other. Many persons have such ability, but there are others who have not mastered the art of being alone with an important other. They express their eagerness to connect by constantly talking or incessantly touching. These persons often find it difficult to be alone under any circumstances, but it is when they are with an important other that their need to avoid the feeling of aloneness is most intense.

It has been said that in a good marriage, each spouse protects the solitude of the other. From this perspective, I am particularly interested in what goes on in relationships that makes it both acceptable and desirable for the partners to be comfortably alone with each other. And I believe that in a very good relationship, times of being alone alternate with periods of connecting.

When one person wishes to interrupt the separateness and connect with his or her partner, but the partner does not respond in ways that lead to a connection, dysynchrony occurs.

And as dysynchrony can lead to either conflict or repair, these periods are crucial minievents in a shared life. Further, the couple's response to the inevitable periods of dysynchrony tends to become patterned. For many, the pattern is one of dysynchrony's leading to conflict; for others, repair is the more frequent outcome.

Repair usually results when partners learn to talk about what is going on between them as it is taking place. As I try to help couples learn this, we focus on two issues that seem to be at the heart of the process of repair. The first is whether the partner wishing to be understood (wishing to connect) sent a clear message of what he or she wanted. If not, he or she is encouraged (and, if necessary, taught) to ask more clearly. The second issue is the failure of the other partner to respond in a way that would lead to connection. This usually means a failure to respond in ways that encourage the other to explore what is on his or her mind. I ask that partner to correct his or her response by taking an exploratory approach. By working in this way, I am trying to help couples develop a patterned response of repair following the inevitable periods of dysynchrony. This circumvents conflict and leads to connection.

There are a number of ways in which the pattern of repair can be learned. The more fortunate couples have learned it on their own. It is an important piece of how relationships can heal.

It is, then, the ability to connect with an important other, as well as to be comfortably alone when with that other, that is central to healing relationships. Of equal importance is the ability to repair our inevitable failures to connect, following those periods of dysynchrony, which, unless repaired, lead to conflict and alienation.

chapter three

Defining the Relationship

When two persons begin to feel that their relationship may be important in their individual futures, the question of what kind of a relationship they are to have becomes the central issue. They begin the complex, mostly unconscious, process of negotiating the basic structure of their relationship, and do so indirectly around the questions that all couples face: how money is to be handled, the circumstances in which affection is to be expressed and the form of that expression, how relationships with their families of origin are to be managed, and the extent to which each may have a life of his or her own, as well as such mundane issues as who takes out the trash and who washes the dishes.

There are more basic relationship issues embedded within these "everyday" matters; most important are how connected (close, intimate) and how separate (independent, autonomous) the partners are to be. All of these issues involve the possibility of agreement (being together or connected) or disagreement (being separate). Disagreement may have several consequences: each partner may clarify better what he or she thinks; each partner may come to respect the other's views; or conflict, with or without escalation and generalization, may result.

WHAT IS CONNECTEDNESS?

Connectedness can be understood as having three parts. The first is commitment, the emotional priority that each partner gives the other. For many persons, the spouse has a higher priority than anyone else, whereas for others, a child, parent, friend, job, hobby, or lover may have greater emotional priority. One can be understood as connected to a person if there is a strong, high-priority commitment. Commitment does not, however, tell us much about the level of closeness in the relationship.

Closeness is the second part of connectedness. It can be understood as the extent to which two persons share values, interests, activities, and friends. Although closeness, defined as sharing, is an important part of connectedness, it does not inform us as to the presence of psychological intimacy.

Psychological intimacy is the mutual sharing of vulnerabilities. It is the ability of the partners to talk directly and openly with each other about very personal experiences and feelings that rarely are discussed with anyone else. Intimacy also involves each partner's listening in ways that lead to feeling understood and safe. A great deal of trust is necessary if there is to be psychological intimacy.

Thus, connectedness comprises commitment, closeness, and intimacy. Two persons can be seen as most strongly connected when all three parts are present.

WHAT IS SEPARATENESS?

Separateness also is understood as having three parts. The first is the capacity of each partner to experience himself or herself as a distinct person with a unique blend of both assets and liabilities. This part of separateness involves the capacity to recognize and express the ways in which one is different from one's partner.

The second part is the ability to function autonomously—to take good care of one's self and to manage one's life effectively independently of others.

The third part involves the capacity for solitude—the ability to be alone and to enjoy the aloneness that is at the heart of solitude.

RECOGNIZING CONNECTEDNESS AND SEPARATENESS

The amount and quality of a couple's connectedness and separateness can be estimated from their answers to questions about each other's importance as compared with other people or activities, how much time the partners share, and how deeply they discuss uncomfortable feelings with each other.

Couples therapists ask questions about commitment, closeness, intimacy, independence, autonomy, and comfort with solitude, and they pay careful attention to the answers, especially those that point to problems that one or both partners have identified.

Descriptions of what the spouses actually *do* in these areas, as compared with what they *say,* often add valuable insight.

Almost any balance of connectedness and separateness will "work," as long as the balance is satisfactory to both partners. Some couples construct a relationship that has high levels of both connectedness and separateness, whereas others negotiate a high-connectedness, low-separateness balance or one that involves low connectedness and high separateness. If both partners are satisfied with the balance, the relationship is likely to go smoothly. If the balance suits one partner but not the other, however, conflict is apt to result. This type of conflict is particularly important because it stems from a disagreement about the basic structure of the relationship. The couple may choose to argue only about money, for example, but the hidden issue most often is the failure to negotiate an agreement about the balance of connectedness and separateness. Although the tension flowing from this conflict about the basic structure of the relationship may erupt only occasionally, it still is there, beneath the surface.

The conflict I encounter most frequently in my marital therapy practice is that in which one spouse wants more connectedness, and, in particular, greater intimacy, than does the other spouse. The other spouse appears satisfied with a balance skewed toward less connectedness and more separateness. It is important to note, however, that the pattern of a pursuer (the spouse seeking greater connectedness) and a pursued (the spouse resisting greater connectedness) may not be as stable as seems at first. In a subset of such couples, the roles are interchangeable. If the pursued stops retreating and becomes more available, the pursuer does not celebrate, but instead avoids the sought-after increased closeness and intimacy. This pattern can be understood as collusive avoidance of connectedness and intimacy.

Our studies at the Timberlawn Research Foundation have demonstrated that couples who negotiate a balance of high connectedness *and* high separateness are most apt to have relationships that are highly satisfactory to both partners, and encourage their maturation, as well as provide an ideal environment in which children can incorporate both sets of skills.

AS TIME GOES BY

Although the initial negotiations around everyday issues early in the relationship are often critical, the process never completely comes to an end. As the partners continue to evolve, their needs for more or less connectedness and separateness may change. Some couples successfully negotiate a new balance, whereas others appear for marital therapy when one partner has initiated efforts to change the balance and is met by resistance from the spouse.

Marshall and Molly reported that after 30 years of marriage, they were arguing more than ever. A history of their relationship revealed a balance of low connectedness and high separateness. Molly was never completely satisfied with the lack of closeness and intimacy with Marshall, but found satisfaction in her relationship with their daughter, Jane. "Jane and I have been very close," she said, "and have always done a great deal together. Last year, for example, we reached the finals of the mother–daughter state tennis doubles tournament. We're really good friends."

When Jane married and moved to a distant state, Molly felt depressed. "I was really lost—I missed her so much." Marshall was busy with a successful career and was often traveling. When home, he was mostly involved in sports. This did not represent any change in their relationship, but with Jane gone, Molly needed more from him. Molly cried a lot; Marshall kept his distance. Molly argued for more trips together; Marshall said he was too busy. Molly began to buy more clothes; Marshall criticized her for "wasting money." Molly frequently would drink too much and then would be openly critical of Marshall; Marshall would retreat further.

They came to see me around Molly's demand that Marshall give her more of himself and his demand that Molly control her drinking and excessive shopping. Beneath the surface of these concerns was a struggle over Molly's attempt to renegotiate a different balance of connectedness and separateness and Marshall's desire to keep things as they were.

There are particular times in the life of a couple that encourage a reworking of the balance—the last child's leaving home, the birth of a child, the retirement of one or both spouses, a new job or a geographic relocation. These are "transitions" that may require changes in the balance in order to accommodate the altered circumstances. Some marital therapists emphasize that couples are most apt to seek treatment when they are "stuck" in such a transition, and cannot come to an agreement that satisfies both. My experience suggests that at the heart of being stuck is the inability to renegotiate the balance of connectedness and separateness.

WHAT DOES EACH PARTNER BRING TO THE NEGOTIATION?

It is important to know that each person enters adult life with a more or less established preference for certain levels of connectedness and separateness. Some are able both to enter close relationships and to function well on their own. Others may function well independently and take good care of themselves, but avoid any semblance of closeness in relationships. Still others may have the capacity for closeness but cannot function autonomously. They often appear to need others excessively, to avoid responsibilities, and to find aloneness very uncomfortable.

BIOLOGICAL FACTORS

An individual's balance of connectedness and separateness is determined by a number of factors. First, it is increasingly recognized that the capacities for both connectedness and separateness are influenced by the relative efficiency and dominance of certain brain systems. Mothers have always known the difference between a baby who is cuddly from the start and one who pushes away. Children who are very shy may have been born with an inherited tendency toward separateness. Other brain systems involved in the balance of an individual's capacity for connectedness and separateness have to do with feelings. In order to connect closely with others, one must be aware of one's own feelings, as well as those of important others, and some persons are born with this capacity.

EARLY EXPERIENCES

Having acknowledged the importance of inherited, "hard-wired" brain systems, it is important to emphasize that these brain systems at first are quite immature and continue to develop after birth. How well or poorly they develop is determined by the infant's early experiences, particularly with the primary caretaker—usually the mother. There is now solid research evidence that everyday experiences in the first year or two of an infant's life result in either a *secure* or an *insecure attachment* to the primary caretaker.

If the primary caretaker (let us say the mother) is able, for the most part, to understand the infant's feelings and needs, and to respond consistently with affectionate, warm, appropriate caretaking, the infant develops *a secure attachment* to her. The infant learns, indelibly, that the mother is a consistent source of nurturance and security.

On the other hand, if the mother generally is insensitive to the infant's feelings and needs (misreads or ignores), and tends to respond in a cold or unaffectionate fashion, the infant develops what is called an *avoidant attachment.*

Mothers who fluctuate inconsistently and unpredictably between warm and sensitive and cold and insensitive instill an ambivalent attachment in the infant—confusion about when and why one can expect to be treated well or badly.

Finally, if the mother is abusive and frightening to the infant, the child's attachment becomes *disorganized* by fearful insecurity.

Unless powerful new relationship experiences intervene, these "inner working models" influence all later relationships. Children with secure attachments find, throughout childhood, adolescence, and adulthood, that both connectedness and separateness come easily.

Children with avoidant attachments unconsciously anticipate being treated coldly and indifferently by others; they protect themselves by avoiding close relationships, learning that compulsive self-reliance is a safer path (low on connection skills, high on the skills of separateness). This style also persists throughout life, unless some form of healing takes place.

Ambivalently attached children, confused about how to feel safe and secure, but knowing that warmth and understanding can sometimes be found, tend, throughout childhood, adolescence, and adulthood, to become compulsively preoccupied with finding these qualities in others or with seducing others into being loving and giving (high on connection skills, low on the unpracticed skills of autonomy).

The most unfortunate infants, exposed to life-threatening hostility and violence, are *disorganized and fearful* in relationships, and are vulnerable to being reclusive, eccentric, bizarre, and sometimes dangerous throughout life, as they perceive little of value in themselves or others.

Thus, an individual's capacities for connectedness and separateness are molded by both heredity and experience. But whatever the result of the interaction between biology and early relationships, there is yet another powerful influence on the child's capacities for connectedness and separateness: the family's "rules."

FAMILY RULES

Families develop unspoken (unconscious) rules about how connected and how separate family members should be. For some families, the rules are that close connections are to be avoided and separateness encouraged. These families emphasize individuality, accomplishments, and successful competition, but discourage the open expression of feelings, sensitivity to the feelings of others, and "family rituals" that emphasize the importance of connections among the family members.

A young lawyer came for individual therapy after his marriage had failed. He suspected that his ex-wife's complaints that he was a loner, unable to be close to others and incapable of intimacy, might be valid. In describing his childhood, he said, "We were a collection of rugged, mostly successful individuals. My parents were never openly affectionate. They had separate interests and friends. They even took separate vacations." When asked about daily routines (family rituals), he said, "We never had meals together—it was everyone fixing whatever he or she wanted and eating alone. Even for big holidays, like Thanksgiving, we were rarely together." When asked about what was most important in his family, he said, "Academics and sports. It was important to beat everybody else, to win. Getting A's and making the varsity were taken for granted. That's what I learned— to be self-sufficient and to compete successfully."

Other families emphasize closeness without an accompanying emphasis on separateness. The family rules discourage independence, important relationships outside the family, and being one's own person. Such families often make it difficult for their members to separate from the family and have lives of their own.

Jack and Sally came for couples therapy early in their marriage because of increasing conflict. Sally's major complaint was that Jack wasn't "there" enough for her. Jack felt that Sally wanted to control him by occupying all of his free time. "She doesn't want me to play golf with friends, see my mother once a week, or go to the Cowboys' games with my brother," Jack reported. Sally's response was that she wouldn't complain about such things if Jack were more available to her emotionally. "I'm never truly the center of his attention," she said, "even when we're alone, he's reading or watching television."

Jack's family had emphasized individuality; Sally's had not. She had grown up in a family that stressed sharing, agreeing on almost everything, and maintaining nearly constant contact with each other. The family rules emphasized an intense connectedness and did not prepare her adequately for being on her own. Jack's family did not prepare him adequately for closeness. How and why two persons with such different family rules came together often relates to each partner's unconscious search for a healing relationship.

Some families have unspoken rules that emphasize both connectedness and separateness. Often these families teach the importance of context and judgment. They believe that some situations call for relating closely to others, whereas others require high levels of independence, and that there are guidelines for deciding which is which. The strength of these families is that they prepare individuals for both relationships with others *and* functioning independently.

Janet was studied at Timberlawn Research Foundation as part of a family research project. In describing her childhood, she said, "In looking back, I think it was a really remarkable experience. My parents had a great marriage—lots of open affection and respect for each other. At the same time, they were very different. Dad was more driven and goal-oriented. Mom, a very successful office manager, was, to a greater extent, the instigator of open affection and the creator of our togetherness. Both of them encouraged us to be open and honest with our feelings and to follow our own paths. We learned from them how to be close—and how to be on our own."

In addition to illustrating family rules that encourage both connectedness and separateness, Janet's description of her family contains another important observation. The rules about relationships and autonomy came directly from the nature of her parents' relationship (they were lived, not just preached).

The levels of connectedness and separateness in one's parents' marriage play an important role in what one brings to the negotiation of the structure of one's own central relationship.

Bringing It All Together

The inherited capacities for connectedness and separateness, their interactions with important attachments in infancy and early childhood, and the nature of family rules regarding them are emphasized because these three sets of general factors are of central importance for most persons in shaping their adult balance of connectedness and separateness. There are, however, special factors that also can influence this balance: the loss of a parent or sibling during childhood, a long illness that inhibits a child's social development, prolonged exposure to parental conflict, neglect or abuse during childhood, and the absence of supportive relationships with siblings, other relatives, or special friends. These general and specific factors usually operate unconsciously by instilling in the developing child deep fears of either closeness or separateness.

FEARS OF CONNECTEDNESS OR SEPARATENESS

Often a person will be aware of the behavior engendered by an inner fear, but not of the fear itself. Thus, a man may acknowledge difficulty with making a commitment to a woman, but not realize that this avoidance flows from inner fears of abandonment. Or a woman may be aware of her pattern of turning down promotions, but be unaware that this stems from the inner fear that rising above the crowd (being separate) is inevitably associated with disapproval and retaliation.

More extreme situations—although also quite common—involve the lack of awareness of *both* the inner fear and the resulting behavior pattern. The man may feel that, although he always stands ready to commit to love, "Women just aren't dependable—they say they love you and then they change their minds for no reason." The woman whom others see as always turning down opportunities for greater responsibilities may feel that she has never been offered anything but "crummy deals." These unconscious mental "tricks" are called "defense mechanisms," and although we pay an exorbitant price when we become excessively dependent on them, in small, judicious doses they protect us from distressing anxiety, guilt, and shame.

Mental health professionals generally agree that, beginning in infancy, the child takes into his or her developing memory system relationships that involve the child and his or her most important others, such as the mother, the father, and siblings. More recently, it has become obvious that the child also takes into the immature memory system early relationships between others to which he or she is exposed, such as the parents' relationships with each other.

Each of these now-internalized relationships is associated with a predominant feeling, and the relationship and the feeling are stored in the still-developing brain of the child. Single traumatic experiences, such as being molested (and the associated feelings), certainly are taken in and stored in the brain. But much more commonly, it is the thousands of repetitive daily interactions with important others and the associated feelings that are stored—for example, repeatedly seeking closeness with a depressed father who is unavailable emotionally, feeling hurt upon being rejected, and coming to fear that reaching out for close relationships will always result in rejection and pain.

All of us seem to have predominant relationship patterns stored in our early memory systems. Such patterns involve a *wish* directed at an important other, the *response of the other*, and our *reaction to that response*. In the example above, the child *wished to feel loved*, the father *responded with rejection*, and the child *reacted by feeling hurt, unimportant, and afraid of closeness.*

These stored relationship patterns may not be—in fact, most often are not—consciously recalled. For many, all that is remembered is the third step: the final reaction. "As long as I can recall," a young physician reported, "I've avoided being too close to others. As a matter of fact, every time I've let my guard down, I've been disappointed." Another pattern is to remember the early experiences, but not the associated feelings. A young woman described (with cool detachment) her distant, unaffectionate mother. When her therapist suggested that her mother's unavailability must have hurt, she replied, "No, I don't think so. That's just the way she was—there was nothing personal about it." No child experiences a cold mother in such a "grown-up" way.

It is also believed that certain situations provoke the return of the deeply hidden feelings. Although some provocations seem obvious (for example, the molested child who as an adult becomes fearful in sexual situations), more often only a rough approximation of the childhood experience will activate the fears. An example is the woman, sexually abused as a child, who becomes highly anxious (without knowing why) when even inadvertent, nonerotic physical contact occurs, such as brushing against a stranger on the sidewalk.

Thus, each partner brings to a deepening relationship a balance of separateness and connectedness that has been determined by a number of factors. The roles of heredity, early attachment experiences, family rules, and inner fears have been emphasized because these are the ones that often are most obvious in the material presented by individuals and couples who come for therapy or volunteer for marital/family research programs.

chapter four

Power: The Dynamics of Connectedness and Separateness

The negotiation of a balance of connectedness and separateness begins early in a relationship. Part of their initial attraction involves each partner's unconscious perception of the other's balance of these needs and skills. But this sensing can be thrown off if there is an early phase of intense mutual infatuation, which may interfere with an accurate appraisal of the loved one. The romantic "high" includes the tendency to see the other in an idealized way. It is possible to mistake extreme dependency in the other, for example, as a capacity to connect without recognizing the flawed autonomy underlying that dependency. It is equally possible to see the other as strong and independent without accurately sensing what actually may be the partner's inability to be close.

Although there are always some trade-offs in any relationship, they become more obvious the better one comes to know the other. One patient discussed her graduate-school romance in the following way: "I really had an unrealistic picture of him until we began to live together. It soon became clear that he wanted me to take care of him—pick up his socks, iron his shirts, do the cooking and dishes, and even be responsible for seeing that he got to classes on time. In class, he was bright, assertive, and very talented. At home, he was a dependent little boy who wanted mothering. When I realized this, I got out of the relationship."

SOME FREQUENT COMBINATIONS

Persons with high levels of the capacity for both connectedness and separateness may be drawn to each other. The negotiation of an acceptable balance is based on determining the areas of their shared life in which they can agree to be together and those in which they can agree to be different. This process involves the ability of each to respect differences, rather than to see them as issues of right or wrong. The long-term outlook for such couples is very positive.

Some individuals with a balance of high separateness/low connectedness have relationships they judge to be very satisfactory. These relationships may seem unusually distant to an outsider who values closeness, but work well for the participants, except that neither learns to be close. A high level of satisfaction with the relationship (usually based on the absence of chronic conflict) is achieved at the expense of becoming capable of greater closeness. Trouble develops if one partner begins to want more closeness from the other, perhaps as a consequence of adult developmental transitions, midlife crises, or the loss of an important relationship with a parent, sibling, child, or best friend.

Persons with a low capacity for separateness may search for spouses who seem to be autonomous. It is as if, like a child, they wish to be taken care of by someone they see as strong. The more autonomous partner may, in turn, be looking for someone to "parent"—a powerful but somewhat distant way to relate to another adult. Both partners may find these relationships very satisfactory, although one often fails to learn greater autonomy and the other fails to learn to be close and intimate. Problems arise if, and when, the more childlike partner decides he or she wants greater power, or if the parental partner tires of carrying most of the burden of adult responsibilities and demands more "grown-up" behavior from the spouse.

When two persons with low capacities for separateness come together, an overly dependent relationship often evolves. Neither seems able to function without the other; their mutual dependence is extreme. Both partners' sense of self is bound up in the relationship. As might be anticipated, separation or the illness or death of one partner can result in overwhelming anxiety for the other.

Understanding the dynamics of the negotiation of the basic balance of connectedness and separateness must begin with an appreciation of the individual balance each partner brings to the relationship. The early negotiations almost always take place around everyday issues. Each partner has his or her own agenda—the way he or she envisions the relationship. Thus, from the start, a process is set in motion in which each tries to persuade the other to form a relationship based on each partner's sense of what is "right" or "the way a relationship ought to be." Many couples therapists thus consider marriage to be an intensely "political" process (in the sense of influencing, guiding, establishing limits and controls, organizing, and governing), and believe that power and the way it is dealt with by the couple are critical in understanding what goes on in a marriage.

POWER IN RELATIONSHIPS

There is no aspect of marriage that is more misunderstood and controversial than the role of power. Consider the common statement that one can have either love or power, but not both—as if the two were antithetical. Nothing could be farther from the truth; indeed, in order to have an enduring love relationship, a couple must deal with the issue of power.

This is not to say that people enter relationships just to obtain power. One does not have to endorse power seeking as an important individual motivation in order to understand its role in human relationships.

THE NEED TO DEAL WITH POWER

Living in enduring relationships is a very complicated process. Life brings much that is unexpected, and is often marked by uncertainty and anxiety. Stress presents itself in many forms. Some types require only temporary accommodation; other forms are ongoing and need major adjustments. When stress is high, we seek a comfortable sense of certainty so that our anxiety does not become unbearable.

One path to certainty is to have a clear "system structure"; that is, to know who is to do what, and to anticipate correctly the responses of important others. These habitual ways of interacting usually become more or less automatic; they do not require deliberate consideration.

Couples and families have a multitude of tasks to perform, thus mandating the establishment of clear and predictable responsibilities, or structure. Power is the influence that brings this structure into being.

If human systems did not develop a structure, life would be chaotic, and the system would be ineffective. This understanding has led students of marriage and the family to the conclusion that a human system cannot *not* organize.

POWER AND THE DEFINITION OF THE RELATIONSHIP

Having decided to become a couple, the partners' main task is to define the basic structure of the relationship. Here, the core issue is the amount and quality of both separateness and connectedness that are to prevail. Each partner brings to the indirect negotiation of the balance of separateness and connectedness a sense of what is "right" and a desire for a relationship that expresses that balance.

It is in the negotiation of this balance that power is so important. Each partner tries to shape the balance in a way that seems comfortable. If the spouses' individual needs for separateness and connectedness are similar, there will be very few problems in defining this feature of an enduring relationship. If, however, they discover that their needs are different, there is apt to be a prolonged, and often conflictual, process of negotiation—a "power struggle."

HOW DOES POWER REVEAL ITSELF?

It would be unlikely for a couple to discuss the structure of their relationship directly. Rather, it is in the deciding of such matters as those relating to sex, money, friends, and families of origin that the issue of power is most evident. When and how to have sex; how money is to be earned, spent, and saved; whether relationships with each spouse's friends from the past are to be continued or dropped; when each spouse's family is to be seen; which activities are to be shared and which are to be done separately—these and other everyday decisions are the areas in which the couple attempts to negotiate agreement, effect compromises, agree to disagree, or continue to argue.

In the process of these negotiations, most couples develop a more or less stable pattern of power distribution in their relationship. However, the pattern may change in response to developmental events or crises, and requires a considerable period of negotiation to redefine it.

PATTERNS OF POWER IN MARRIAGES

Scientific studies at the Timberlawn Research Foundation have identified four main patterns of power distribution in marriage: egalitarian, dominant–submissive, conflicted, and chaotic.

EGALITARIAN

The egalitarian pattern is characterized by relatively equal sharing of power. Both spouses exert influence on all decisions, including the balance of separateness and connectedness. This pattern may seem natural for some couples, but for others, long, often painful negotiation is required to achieve equality.

Couples with this type of power distribution may agree to participate equally in all important decisions, or may divide areas of responsibility. Because of the equal power, there is greater likelihood that the partners will respect each other's opinions and beliefs. Trust comes easily and psychological intimacy is possible. There are no rigid gender roles, but rather a freedom to share responsibilities according to skills and interests.

Because the consequences of equal power influence all aspects of the marriage, it is not surprising that our research findings demonstrate that couples with relatively equal power most often have high levels of marital satisfaction and are likely to raise emotionally healthy children who are capable of both autonomy and closeness.

DOMINANT–SUBMISSIVE

The dominant–submissive pattern is perhaps the most common in our culture. One spouse clearly has greater influence in defining the balance of separateness and connectedness. That this pattern is most often seen in husband-dominated relationships may reflect a mainstream "traditional" arrangement, but also can be influenced by ethnic tradition: some ethnic or cultural groups continue to regard husband dominance as the only "normal" or "proper" marriage.

The dominant–submissive pattern may be complementary, that is, satisfactory to both spouses, or there may be an undercurrent of tension and conflict. When there is conflict, it most often stems from the less powerful spouse's resentment at not having enough influence in decision making, but sometimes it springs from the more powerful spouse's resenting having to bear the burden of responsibility for all decisions.

Whether complementary or conflicted, dominant–submissive marriages have some built-in disadvantages. It is difficult or impossible, for example, to be open, honest, and direct about one's ideas, fears, wishes, or needs with another who has extreme power over you, or with a partner who is seen as powerless and, therefore, as irresponsible.

Although dominant–submissive relationships may be remarkably stable over time, there is a considerable loss of flexibility in decision making. The input of the submissive spouse is often overlooked in the process, and control of the couple's life together is too much in the hands of one person. The balance of separateness and connectedness is decided by the dominant spouse's needs, and when the couple seeks therapy, the relationship is seen as skewed heavily in the direction of high separateness and low connectedness. Submissive spouses often complain of the lack of closeness and intimacy, but without understanding that they have given away their right to cooperate in deciding the level and quality of connectedness by their participating in the formation of a dominant–submissive relationship.

Marital therapists commonly see dominant–submissive couples either when the submissive spouse develops symptoms (depression and substance abuse are common) or when a child exhibits school or behavioral problems.

CONFLICTED

The conflicted pattern of power distribution is the one most commonly seen in therapists' offices. Either from the start of the relationship or later around developmental challenges or crises, the spouses engage in ongoing and repetitive battles. Some couples argue only about one subject—such as money, sex, families of origin, or raising the children. Other conflicted couples fight about almost every aspect of their relationship. For some, the conflicts are constantly present. For others, periods of truce are interrupted periodically by bitter conflicts.

At the core of the problem in conflicted marriages is the inability of the spouses to agree on the balance of separateness and connectedness. In most cases, there is a strong possibility that both spouses have underlying fears of too much closeness. Conflict produces distance, within the context of connection. Often a period of shared closeness will stir up one or both partners' underlying fears of closeness and provoke extreme conflict.

If intense and pervasive, conflict has adverse consequences for both of the spouses. Moreover, there is now solid evidence that exposure to parental conflict has a harmful effect on the children—consequences that can be detected both physically and psychologically by age three or four, and may be lifelong.

CHAOTIC

In the chaotic pattern, neither spouse appears willing or able to provide effective leadership. For some couples, this reflects a relationship that is so distant, unconnected, or alienated that emotional contact does not occur. Each spouse goes his or her separate way, and the marriage has no direction and no sense of teamwork.

In a second type of chaotic marriage, the opposite dynamic operates. The spouses are so tightly bound together, so afraid of separateness, that effective joint decision making is impossible. The need always to agree is so strong that circumstances are apt to rule; there is no real attempt to provide any sense of direction for fear that a difference or disagreement might arise.

The chaotic pattern of marriage is associated with the failure of the development of connectedness or separateness and the lack of effective leadership, leading to severe problems for the couple, and for their children as well.

These four patterns of power distribution can be understood as different approaches to the attempt to negotiate a balance of separateness and connectedness. No aspect of the definition of an enduring relationship is more important than how the spouses deal with power. Partners either share power, construct a skewed relationship with unequal power, fight over power, or refuse to acknowledge the relevance of power. Invoking each of these patterns has its own consequences, both for the relationship itself, and for the children growing up in the family, and whether they will learn how to negotiate power (or how not to), will seek out or fear closeness, or will enjoy or flee from responsibilities.

chapter five

———————— ❧ ————————

Carrying the Past Into the Present

Before exploring the themes that the developing child has stored in his or her immature memory system and brings into adult relationships, it is necessary to look at the current debate as to whether childhood memories are always the accurate recall of actual experiences or can be reconstructions based on something other than such experiences.

RECOLLECTIONS AND RECONSTRUCTIONS

The difficulty in sorting out accurate recollections from less accurate, or even imaginary, reconstructions is nowhere better illustrated than at family reunions.

Two brothers in their 70s were discussing an accident that occurred when one was seven and the other five.

Older Brother: "I can remember it so clearly. The ice truck backed out and ran over Jimmy. I can still hear his leg breaking and his screams."

Younger Brother: "That's not the way it happened. The ice truck didn't have anything to do with it. It was still in the driveway. Jimmy ran out from the side of it into the street and got hit by old Bankston driving his Packard."

Older Brother: "That's pure bull. Old Bankston just happened to be driving by and heard the screaming. He stopped to help."

Younger Brother: "Hey, I was there and closer to it than you were. I *know* exactly what happened."

Whatever really happened is impossible to know. Both brothers likely have combined early memories with later reconstructions to form stories that are coherent and the truth of which each is convinced. This difference in the recall of shared experiences is so common that many students of early memory have accepted the idea that there are two types of truth: historical and narrative.

Under most circumstances, well-trained therapists accept the idea that all early memories are in part accurate recollections and in part inaccurate reconstructions. Most often, therapists are more interested in the *central themes* embedded in childhood memories and what those themes reflect (the narrative truth) than in the "real" facts versus the unintended fabrications. Therapists know that there is no foolproof way to separate memories of early actual experiences from subsequent reconstructions. It is only when a legal or moral issue is raised concerning how someone was abused as a child that the issue of accurate recall versus reconstruction becomes charged with strong emotion.

THE NATURE OF THE EXPERIENCE

Because the brain is so immature at birth, it has been widely held that there is a normal amnesia for the first two years or more of life experiences. More recent research, however, suggests that the newborn's brain is capable both of perceiving certain differences (e.g., recognizing the mother's sound, smell, and face) and of storing those impressions for future use. Thus, we do not always know exactly what to make of those persons who claim to recall experiences from the first few years of life. Clinicians, who are more interested in the *themes* of such memories than in their factual basis, may tend to emphasize the reconstructed nature of very early memories, but the truth is that we don't know what they represent in every case.

The age at which an experience takes place is an influential factor. The older the child when it happens, the more likely it is that the recollection of the circumstances has a stronger base in actual experience. Even for later experiences, however, there is often much difference in recall by those who shared them.

There are two other important factors that contribute to the nature of the experience. One is the relative importance of single traumatic events versus repetitive patterns of harmful relationships. How does one understand the effect of a single trauma of a violent or sexual nature as contrasted with the impact of day-after-day, year-after-year emotional rejection by a depressed, withdrawn parent? The complexity of such comparisons is overwhelming. We do know, however, that both episodes and patterns may damage the child's developing sense of a coherent self and the growth of adequate self-esteem.

Another issue is the amount of emotional arousal involved. The clinician's usual "rule of thumb" is that some degree of emotional arousal is required for an experience to be registered in the child's developing memory system. If, however, the emotional arousal is extreme, the emotions and/or the experience itself may be blocked from consciousness. This is what is meant by "repressed" memories.

REPRESSED MEMORIES

There is little doubt that some events, particularly those of a very painful nature, can be forgotten but still stored somewhere in the brain. As an adult, one may not recall early abuse even though it was well documented by others, and its memory can remain repressed (forgotten) for many years. It is the pain-relieving function of such forgetting that led early students of such memories to understand this type of forgetting as an unconscious defense against unbearable pain. It is also true that repressed memories may play a role in the development of some psychiatric symptoms. Recapturing the repressed memories can be part of the process of recovering from such symptoms.

To complicate matters further, we know that recovery from symptoms can take place without the recall of forgotten memories, but also that some patients' symptoms have worsened considerably following what appears to be the "return" of previously repressed experiences.

Another, very difficult issue in the rediscovery of repressed memories is the extent to which another person, such as a therapist, suggests to or convinces the patient that he or she has such memories and that they are the accurate recall of actual experiences. This has been called "implanting," and research evidence exists to the effect that implanting memories—even for events that are known never to have happened—is not difficult to do.

IMPLANTED MEMORIES

If parents tell a young child several times that something has happened, the child often will incorporate the event into his or her developing memory systems—whether or not the story was true. If, for example, a child is told a fictitious story about his or her getting lost in a shopping mall several years earlier, the experience may be recounted as an actual event in subsequent interviews.

There also is research evidence of the successful implantation of memories in adults. In addition, a growing number of former psychotherapy patients have recanted their memories of childhood abuse by a parent. These memories were "uncovered" during their therapy and, at a later point, they accused their therapists of implanting them. Several therapists have been successfully sued by the parents of former patients for implanting false memories of abuse.

There is no escaping the fact that a lucrative industry has grown up around the "uncovering" of "memories" of abuse, often through "treatment" programs directed by poorly trained professionals (or nonprofessionals) who rely on group pressure and hypnotic techniques.

SCREEN MEMORIES

There is also the intriguing issue of why one remembers some experiences and not others. We are a long way from understanding everything involved, but one factor is what is known as "screen" memories. Early psychoanalytic observations revealed that some patients focus on certain early memories in an effort to block from consciousness other memories that may be even more distressing. For example, a man may focus on early memories of neglect suffered at the hands of a live-in baby sitter. The recall of these experiences may shield him from a much more painful memory, of his mother's neglect. The screen memory serves to "screen out" the more painful reality, while portraying the equally true narrative theme (neglect by a caretaker).

ALTERED MEMORIES

To further complicate our understanding of memories of childhood is the process of changing early memories to adapt better to the present. It appears that many memories may be unconsciously altered in order to deal with present circumstances. A recent demonstration of this process involves research from the Timberlawn Research Foundation.

During their first pregnancy, some women who initially rated their fathers as warm and supportive during their childhoods *changed their ratings to negative* after four years of parenting their own first children. The negative change was not associated with any ascertainable characteristics of the women or their fathers. Rather, the women's changed opinions of their fathers seemed to be directly related to changes in their husbands! These husbands had become mildly depressed and were not very effective parents. The women, however, continued to rate their marriages as satisfactory. It appears that they changed their previously positive memories of their fathers in order to bolster the belief that their marriages were satisfactory, even though their husbands were depressed and not parenting well.

This research documents what some students of memory believe is a common occurrence. Memories are revised unconsciously in order to help deal with present circumstances. This takes place outside of awareness, and, if confronted with the change, the person often evinces strong, genuine disbelief and denial.

CERTAINTY ABOUT MEMORIES

The factors noted suggest that one should be very tentative about the real facts of one's childhood. Nevertheless, most persons are convinced that their recollections are based on actual experiences. Indeed, if presented with hard evidence that their memories have changed—for example, if their earlier recordings of memories differ from their current recollections—they often will discount or discredit the evidence. Most persons need to believe that their lives and their memories are coherent and constant, even in the face of strong evidence to the contrary.

AND SO—

The issue, then, is what to make of early memories, both one's own and those of important others. Whether memories of childhood are mostly accurate recollections of actual experiences or mainly inaccurate reconstructions (or, more often, combinations), they are important statements about an individual and his or her sense of self. They may contain the earliest beginnings of what are often ongoing major themes in one's life. They reflect some combination of experience, denial, wishes, and hope. As such, they are the foundation of a sense of self, and should always be taken as important statements about the individual and his or her life.

PROMINENT THEMES FROM EARLY CHILDHOOD MEMORIES

In the clinical setting, I ask patients to describe their families as they were during childhood. After exploring whatever I am told, I ask a series of more focused questions about parents, siblings, relationships, and roles. This is done to develop some understanding of these important features of the patient's story, including:

1. The central relationship themes of the patient's childhood.

2. Needs the patient had that were unfulfilled.

3. The particular role the patient played in the family.

With candidates for professional training, my approach is different. I ask them, "What is it like to be you?" About half respond by sharing their life story, beginning with their childhood family. After listening quietly, I ask clarifying questions. The other half of this sample describe themselves in categorical terms ("I'm ambitious, hard-working, and sensitive"), and I must take the lead in gleaning information about their childhood.

A few patients, and perhaps a third of the professional-training candidates, describe warm, loving families in which both closeness and independence were emphasized. Some nine out of ten patients, and about two thirds of the candidates, recall clearly dysfunctional families, highly problematic early relationship patterns, and/or the acceptance of family roles that interfered with healthy development.

There is no reliable information, however, on the frequency of such findings in a truly representative population. We simply do not know whether there are 10, 20, or 100 such basic themes. Further, my estimates of dysfunctional families of origin for about 90 percent of patients and two thirds of training candidates may be misleading in that both groups may have been responding with what they thought I wanted to hear.

But recent research findings, using a questionnaire approach with college students, identified most of the same themes I have heard from patients and candidates. These themes of painful relationship patterns beginning in the family in early childhood may be called central problematic relationships. They are the core of what must be worked through if an adult relationship is to be healthy.

CENTRAL PROBLEMATIC RELATIONSHIPS

There are scores of possible problematic childhood relationship patterns, each with gradations from mild to severe, and so it is helpful to group them into a small number of basic patterns.

Such patterns most often relate to the child's relationship with his or her mother, father, or other primary caretaker. Sometimes they involve the child, the mother, and the father simultaneously.

Following are the five patterns encountered most often.

1. The perception of close relationships as dangerous

The parent is remembered as abusive, or rejecting, or as abandoning the child through divorce, desertion, or death. Often the parent appears to have been alcoholic or chronically depressed or to have had a striking lack of interest in the child. In other situations, the parent is recalled as cold, insensitive, or caught up in destructive conflicts with the other parent.

For whatever reasons, the parent did not meet the young child's needs for nurturance, physical safety, emotional security, and understanding. The destructive impact on the child may have been buffered, in part, by the other parent, a sibling, or another adult who offered a more secure attachment. The failure of the other parent to protect the child from abuse or rejection, however, often results in a second central problematic relationship of childhood.

For the child, the most common result is the registration of this relationship pattern in the immature memory system as a part of the developing sense of self (who I am, how good or bad I am, how lovable I am, what I am worth). *The central theme becomes the distrust and fear of close relationships or of any form of vulnerability.* The child unconsciously learns to anticipate that closeness and vulnerability will create a major risk of abuse, rejection, or abandonment. As a consequence, there is a strong likelihood that the child will develop one of several self-protective styles of relating to others throughout childhood, adolescence, and adulthood.

A common self-protective style is avoidance. If not tempered by subsequent positive relationships, the child develops into a distant, aloof, suspicious, or angry adult who avoids the risk of being hurt again.

A second style is perfectionism. Here, the individual strives to control the self and the world by always being right. In relationships, this is demonstrated by efforts to control, to exert dominance, and a tendency to suspect the motives of others.

A third, less self-defeating style is caretaking. The child becomes the parent early in life, preoccupied with pleasing others by being the good caretaker. In this way, the child assumes control in important relationships, and, in particular, is able to keep enough distance to avoid vulnerability.

At the core of this relationship pattern is the unconscious fear that close connections are dangerous and are to be avoided. If a subsequent adult relationship is to have a healing impact, it is the fear of closeness that must be overcome.

2. The perception that separateness is dangerous

The parent is remembered as controlling, dominating, intrusive, or overly protective. As a consequence, the child's need to develop a sense of a separate self, independence, and autonomy is compromised. *Separateness, which includes being assertive and exploring on one's own, becomes associated with crippling anxiety.* Often the parent binds the child to herself or himself to compensate for an unsatisfactory marriage.

The parent may be recalled as being controlling in all of his or her relationships, but the effect on the developing child is an impaired capacity for acting independently. Some children with this pattern remain childlike and "helpless" throughout life; others become extremely rebellious in adolescence and young adulthood, rejecting the family's (and society's) rules and values in a poorly orchestrated attempt to gain independence from the controlling parent. This is called the "pseudoindependent" pattern.

Those who deeply fear being on their own often undergo greater than normal "separation anxiety," including panic attacks.

Several types of responses to the controlling parent can become adult relationship styles. In addition to the overly dependent and the pseudoindependent, a third style is that of repetitive failure. In this pattern, the individual makes periodic attempts to function independently at work or in love, but always manages to sabotage himself or herself, thereby unconsciously maintaining the dependent position. A fourth style is approval seeking (or "people pleasing"), in which the effort to please others is exaggerated and is used unconsciously to maintain the dependent position.

Individuals with the "separateness is dangerous" central relationship pattern often evidence conflict—usually between the cultural emphasis on independence and the individual's fearful dependency.

If an adult relationship is to have a healing effect, the fear of separateness must be worked through.

3. Entitlement

The parent may be remembered as overly permissive and as failing to establish appropriate expectations and limits, making the child the focus of her or his emotional world and attempting to gratify every wish. This may occur because of the parent's preoccupation with his or her own importance, or because he or she is alienated from other important relationships and needs the child's total devotion. In some instances, the other parent is disregarded or openly depreciated by the self-centered and self-important parent.

For whatever reason, the parent fails to provide the developing child with a clear structure of reality. *This leads to the child's developing a sense of self that disregards limits and is pervasively "entitled."* That is, other persons' needs are seen as insignificant; all that is important is that the individual have his or her way. As a consequence, such individuals seek self-sacrificing others who can be dominated and used. They most commonly are seen in the role of the *prince* or *princess*, although they also can assume that of the *rule breaker*, whose predominant characteristic is a lack of respect for rules of any sort. A "prince" or "princess" can be a "rule breaker" as well ("I'm entitled to do anything I want to do").

If a subsequent adult relationship is to have a healing impact, it must overcome the intense need to be special and the underlying vague fear that otherwise one is nothing. The individual must become more aware of and sensitive to the needs of others. He or she must develop the capacity for healthy guilt and the consequent ability to observe limits and rules.

4. Disturbances of conscience

The parent, usually the father, is remembered as unavailable or unreliable, often physically, but also, and of equal importance, emotionally. Or the parent is available to the child but clearly disrespects the rules and the needs of others.

In this relationship pattern, the parent does not provide the developing child with a model of a mature conscience. *As an adult, such a child comes to operate without guilt and, most often, his or her only restraint is the fear of punishment.*

In adult relationships, the person is manipulative and exploitative. He or she usually is unable to make lasting commitments to others and is likely to show a relationship pattern of multiple brief involvements in which the other is used and then discarded. Some use seductiveness and manipulation to achieve success in vocations, such as entertainment and politics, where these techniques are valued.

It is not unusual for a person with a disturbed conscience to enter into a relationship with a caretaking "saint," in which a basic dynamic of good and evil, "saint" and "sinner," is established. This relationship provides a long-suffering caretaker for the sinner, who needs a lot of taking care of, and an always available mess for the saint to clean up.

Most often, individuals with disturbances of conscience deeply fear closeness and commitment (having learned that they make you a "patsy"). Others are to be used for one's own needs, but intimacy is to be avoided because the world is dangerous.

If an adult relationship is to have a healing effect, it must demonstrate that closeness and vulnerability can be safe, and that respect for the needs of others is critical to one's genuine security.

5. Disturbances of competition

The parents are remembered as conflicted, alienated from each other, or separated, and the child is involved in an intense relationship with one parent that provides that parent with gratification that substitutes for what is lacking in the troubled marriage.

The child is understood as having won the love of one parent away from the other parent, and so develops into an adult who is either excessively competitive or avoids any and all competition. He or she may unconsciously fear retaliation (based on a dim awareness of the defeated parent's rage) and thus avoids closeness or commitments. Another relationship style is to seek to create "triangles," in which the individual always has a rival (thus repeating the childhood drama). Love is felt not to be possible unless a rival is defeated. Once the rival is defeated, however, another relationship involving a third party is sought.

The adult relationship patterns that may stem from this central problematic relationship of childhood include the intense competitor, the avoider of competition, and the triangulator. The underlying fear is of connections, because important connections provoke unconscious expectations of being punished by the vanquished rival.

If an adult relationship is to have healing impact, it must address the underlying fears of closeness.

COMBINATIONS OF PROBLEMATIC RELATIONSHIP PATTERNS

It is not unusual to find in one person two or more of the types of problematic relationships outlined here. An example is the daughter who is abused and rejected by her alcoholic mother. Her father's attempts to protect her are only partially successful, but she becomes the "apple of his eye" and their relationship replaces his failed marriage. Another example is the son of a dominant, controlling father whose fears of separateness from the father justify repetitive failures and subsequent dependency. The son, however, is also his mother's favorite and develops an incapacitating sense of entitlement.

MISSING INGREDIENTS IN THE FAMILY

There are individuals who do *not* present a clear story of central problematic relationships of childhood, but rather describe childhood families in which something essential to normal development was missing. The two most common missing ingredients are strong, affectionate connections and the encouragement of separateness.

1. Absence of strong connections

Families vary regarding the emphasis they place on open affection, the sharing of feelings, sensitivity to each other's needs, and the use of rituals that symbolically celebrate the sense of family. Some families are very clear that these "family values" are primary; for others, such values are not emphasized.

A sizable number of patients and training candidates describe their childhood families as lacking any strong sense of connectedness. One of two characteristics most often stands out. The first is a distant relationship between the parents, a separateness, that serves as a template for the family as a whole.

The second characteristic is an unusually strong emphasis (in the family "rules") on separateness, independence, and competition. In such families, this focus is so powerful that any sense of affectionate connection within the family is avoided or must be kept secret.

An observation from my clinical work suggests that spouses who experience a deficiency of connectedness in their childhood families are less afraid of closeness and intimacy in adulthood than are those whose fears of closeness are based on a central problematic relationship. Often these "closeness-deficient" persons respond more readily to therapy that involves direct teaching of the conversational approach to intimacy.

It is obvious that, in this situation, a healing marriage means learning how to be close and vulnerable.

2. Absence of an emphasis on separateness

Although not rare, families that fail to emphasize separateness are less frequent in my practice. Such families often can be characterized as "glued together" families that actively discourage separateness. Going out into the world is viewed as dangerous. Differences among family members are minimized, and "we-ness" is the rule. As anticipated, many children from such families have difficulty with separateness. They may also have difficulty entering into new relationships that require a high level of commitment.

When persons from these families develop psychiatric difficulties, the problems are apt to be severe in the sense that they involve the absence of a clear sense of self apart from relationships in the family of origin. Thus, unlike persons from families that fail to teach connectedness, the members of stuck-together families have great difficulty learning how to live successfully away from home at any age.

It is obvious that if adult healing is to occur, this spouse must receive a great deal of encouragement and support for separateness, independence, and autonomy.

NARROW FAMILY ROLES

The assignment and acceptance of a special narrow role in the family are almost always understood to have negative consequences for a child, even if the role appears to be a positive one. The role of "bad" or defective child, if accepted by the child as part of the basic sense of self, may haunt the person throughout life. Even the role of "good" or special child may restrict the development of a well-rounded sense of self, and thus deprive the person of developing his or her unique and genuine personal characteristics.

A large number of special family roles are noted by family therapists; these can be divided into those that appear to be more positive and those that carry an openly negative meaning.

1. Roles with positive meaning

The various "positive" roles all involve a specialness that is valued by at least one parent—those of the good child, the achiever, the prince or princess, the caretaker.

The *good child* may suffer because he or she grows up with the belief that "goodness" is always required. This may lead to an endless quest for perfection, the avoidance of "negative" emotions (such as anger) at all costs (even when appropriate), and deep guilt over the awareness of hidden imperfections. Blandness, a lack of normal assertiveness, and depression are often the price of enforced goodness.

The *achiever* is likely to grow up believing that his or her self-worth is totally contingent on accomplishments; that is, that he or she has no intrinsic worth. Some such children become "workaholics" as adults, always striving to achieve some new goal that presumably will strengthen their shaky self-esteem (but rarely does so for long).

The *prince* or *princess* role is most apt to involve the child's developing into an adult with a strong sense of entitlement. Often such adults have difficulty, both in love and at work, because of their inability to give to others, to share, or to express remorse and gratitude. They value others only insofar as those others provide unlimited emotional and material resources.

The *caretaker* is selected to do for others within the family, often including the assumption of parental responsibilities at a very young age. Such children are apt to project a selfless, "saintly" quality. The assignment and acceptance of this role usually force the youngster to miss experiences of childhood and adolescence that would aid in the development of a well-rounded person. In adulthood, many caretakers search out spouses and others who have disabilities or special physical or emotional needs. This childhood role was one of the more frequently reported by physicians, dentists, and psychotherapists who came to me for either individual or couples therapy.

2. Roles with negative meaning

These role assignments are notoriously destructive of healthy self-esteem. The sense of self comes to center around badness, rebellion, failure, and incompetence. Common types include the scapegoat or bad seed, the underachiever, and the outsider.

As a child, the *scapegoat* or *bad seed* represents the hidden badness in one or both parents. He or she is seen as the cause of all misfortunes that the family experiences. Other children in the family often have opposite role assignments, such as that of the good child or the prince or princess. It does not take long for scapegoated children to begin to behave in keeping with the assignment. The more negative the parents' expectations, the more negative is the child's behavior; the more negative the child's behavior, the more negative are the parents' expectations. As adults, they often present a track record of failure; some criminals were family scapegoats in childhood.

The label of "underachiever" can be a thin disguise for a clearly negative label, "the lazy child" or "the child who doesn't care." This role assignment is often found in families in which one or more other members are high achievers. The adult consequences of the underachiever role include never attaining academic or vocational success, settling for less than is possible in love and work, and having one's sense of self invaded by feelings of incompetence, failure, and shame.

In the *outsider* role, the child maintains a greater distance from the family than other members do, and from its values, traditions, and rituals. Often this assignment is made to keep the parents' excessive dependency on each other from being eroded by the closeness of one parent to the child. Such children may, as adults, occupy marginal positions in their own marriages and work settings.

COMBINATIONS OF THEMES

It is common to find some variant of these themes in the history of childhood relationships. A man, for example, reveals a central problematic relationship with an abusive, alcoholic father. This relationship was embedded in a family structure marked by open conflict and little display of affection. As a child, the man acted as caretaker for his abused mother and younger siblings. His avoidance of closeness as an adult is understood as resulting from his underlying fear of abuse (originally from his father), the lack of any family model of affection and sensitivity, and the acceptance of the caretaking role, which, in part, is an unconscious attempt to avoid vulnerability and maintain control over others.

CONSEQUENCES OF CHILDHOOD THEMES

Several such consequences can be viewed as particularly important. First, the central problematic relationship from childhood, the deficiencies in what the family provided, and special roles within the family are taken into and become part of the child's developing sense of self. They become a basic, unquestioned part of "who I am." This blueprint of who we are, how much we are worth, what we are to expect from others, whom we can trust, and what we must fear and avoid is almost permanent, and is laid down by a process that is mostly outside our conscious awareness.

A second consequence is that these now "internalized" relationships, deficits, and roles are brought into play in important adult relationships. It is in these new relationships that the maladaptive aspects of the inner blueprint are most obvious. The man described above may function well as a surgeon or attorney, but his avoidance of closeness will shape both his choice of important others (including his spouse) and the construction of those relationships.

A third consequence is that these internalizations from childhood experiences are very difficult to eradicate. Mere knowledge does not suffice.

Once one's sense of self is established—usually by early childhood—it is resistant to change. Why is this so?

First, the central problematic relationships, family deficits, role assignments, and inherited biological and neurological factors that work together to create your childhood sense of self are almost invisible to the immature and undiscerning child's mind. You don't know enough as a child to understand how you are being formed and molded.

Second, to the degree that you become aware of any of these influences, you tend to view them as "normal," since the only childhood you know well is your own.

Third, your biological capabilities, central relationship patterns, deficits, and roles *determine* what kind of relationships you can have, and automatically make it impossible in many cases, and difficult in all cases, for you to have the kind of relationship experiences that would be healing.

The shy, avoidant child resists becoming close enough to anyone to have the shyness "cured." The mistrustful and suspicious youngster radiates those qualities, thereby "pushing away" anyone who might be helpful. The same behaviors that protected the child in early life now interfere with the needed healing.

Finally, self-understanding, followed by attempts to change one's ways of relating to others, is no easier to accomplish than is recovering from an addiction or losing excess weight. These major changes in behavioral patterns all may work smoothly for a short time, but quickly lead to such intense discomfort that "relapse" is frequent, and often permanent.

What is required is the development of an intense relationship that lasts a long time and provides the leverage for change in the deep inner sense of self. The three types of intense connections that are the most common avenues of such change are:

1. The healing marriage

2. Psychotherapy

3. The development of a new belief system (often of a religious nature) through a healing relationship with an actual or supernatural other.

chapter six

~

What Kind of Marriage
Do You Have?

Different people judge their marriages very differently. For example, as an intern, I saw the same woman in the emergency room of a Boston hospital on a number of Friday nights. On each occasion, she had been beaten by her drunken husband. When I asked her why she put up with the frequent beatings, she shook her finger at me and said, "You're young and probably have spent most of your life in school, but I'll tell you this—I've got a very good marriage."

Although this example may be extreme, many people stay in relationships that seem to others to be clearly dysfunctional, and yet they report being satisfied. So what does it mean when someone maintains that his or her marriage is "fine"? We all use different yardsticks.

HOW CAN YOU TELL IF A MARRIAGE WORKS?

One must start with a clear definition of what it is that a marriage "should" do. This is no easy matter because there are many different possibilities to consider. A marriage should provide its participants with the physical necessities of food and shelter. It should afford an emotional environment in which healthy individual development is encouraged. It should afford a haven to which one can return when work is done. It should establish a setting in which values are learned. It should be the place where closeness and safety are available. It should also prepare the family members to go out into the world with confidence. The list could go on and on, but at the core of the matter is our understanding that successful adaptive functioning involves both the ability to connect closely with a few significant others and the capacity to be separate. Thus, closeness, commitment, intimacy, separateness, independence, and autonomy are the essence of individual psychological health. It is also clear that these important individual characteristics are the result of many factors, including heredity, early developmental experiences, and the nature of one's marriage and family.

Along with many other marital and family researchers, we define marriage in terms of what it should do for its participants. A healthy marriage should encourage both spouses to continue to develop the twin capacities for closeness and separateness. It should also furnish an environment in which children learn both to relate closely to others and to stand on their own feet. To the extent that a marriage accomplishes these goals, it can be understood as healthy. To the extent that it fails in one or both, it can be considered dysfunctional.

But isn't it true that healthy individuals produce healthy marriages? The answer is a qualified "Yes." Although two psychologically healthy persons may have an increased probability of constructing a healthy marriage, it is far from a sure bet. Some healthy individuals construct clearly dysfunctional marriages. Some healthy marriages, on the other hand, are put together by one healthy individual and one who is not so healthy. Thus, it appears that a healthy marriage requires that at least one of the spouses have a significant level of psychological health.

Perhaps the best answer to this question is: Two healthy partners have the best chance of having a healthy marriage, although one healthy partner is sometimes sufficient (if the other partner is not too deeply disturbed). Moreover, a healthy marriage (however formed) increases the chances that both partners will become healthier.

THE RESEARCH STUDY GROUPS

Although a good deal of what I have learned about healthy and dysfunctional marriages comes from my psychotherapeutic work with couples and families, the findings presented here are based on our studies of research volunteers at the Timberlawn Research Foundation. They came to us from many sources: Some volunteered out of gratitude for a family member's successful therapy, and others after learning about our studies from a doctor, a religious leader, or a friend who was a mental health professional. Still others came after hearing presentations of our work by members of the research team. Some were selected by community groups that identified them as strong or capable families.

Those who came to the studies also had various motivations. Some were intrigued by the idea of healthy marriages. Many wanted to learn something valuable about themselves. Others became interested out of a sense of mission. A few came because they were in pain and wanted help. Not all of them proved to have healthy marriages; indeed, only about 25 percent were rated as healthy.

How representative of the country were these research volunteer couples and families? We can't really say, but do know that they were a diverse group. They were white, African-American, and Mexican-American; wealthy, middle class, and lower income. Some were doctoral-level professionals, many were college graduates, and others had not finished high school. Although most represented the three major religious orientations, some had no formal religious identification. In two of our projects, the couples had at least one adolescent child. In another project, the couple was expecting their first child at the time they were initially studied and were followed by us until that child was in first grade.

How Were They Studied?

It is possible that people who volunteer for such research projects will tell you only what they think you want to hear or will minimize their relationship problems. The solution is not only to set up multiple sessions with them and to listen closely to what they say, but also to use research techniques that do not rely only on what couples can or will tell you about their relationships. This can be accomplished by studying *how* they communicate with each other. Along with other researchers of marital and family systems, we record (with their permission) their responses to problems they are asked to solve, for instance, "What would you like to change about your relationship?" and "What is the most painful loss you've had to deal with?" Instead of focusing only on *what* they say, we rate a wide group of communication variables. Examples: Who provides leadership for the discussion? How much conflict becomes apparent and how is it dealt with? What happens if strong feelings are expressed? Who interrupts whom? How much affection is apparent? Is there respect for each other's beliefs and feelings? Since the couples do not know what we are measuring (usually inferring that we are interested only in the content of their answers), there is little opportunity for them to present a false picture of their skills and deficits.

We use a large number of different approaches to get at the basic structure of the marriage. Among these are extensive individual, couple, and family interviews, as well as paper-and-pencil tests, including psychological tests. Family-of-origin histories are obtained from the adults. We rely heavily on analyses of communication as noted above. Some of these techniques are used at the Foundation, but we also go to the volunteers' homes to obtain information. Many of the interviews and interactional tasks are videotaped for later study by the research team.

The factors that we found to be of central importance in understanding marital and family functioning have been used to construct a group of rating scales. These scales are most often used by therapists and researchers after observing a couple or family discussion. But in my practice, another use of the scales also has proved of value. Each partner is asked to use the scales to rate their marriage. They are to do so privately and then to share their independent ratings with each other. I ask them to discuss the ways in which they differ in their ratings of their marriage. Such discussions can help the couple to identify problem areas and may lead to new learning.

I have also had couples fill out the rating scales for a second time at the end of therapy. This may help both to underscore their gains and to point out areas on which they must continue to work after the cessation of therapy.

The scales are included here as an appendix for those readers who are interested in the factors themselves, or who may wish to use them in rating their own marriages.

We utilize a wide variety of techniques, and our findings are similar to those of other research groups using many different approaches. The consistency of the results of our carefully designed research projects and the fact that our conclusions are corroborated by other well-respected research groups inspire confidence that the descriptions that follow are accurate and useful.

HEALTHY MARRIAGES

Jason and Emily, both teachers, were in their late 20s. They volunteered for our study when Emily was pregnant with their first child. A quiet couple, they enjoyed reading and listening to both jazz and classical music. Their social life revolved around a small group of friends from college and several couples who were members of their Sunday School class at a mainstream Protestant church. They continued to be much involved with their families. Both Jason and Emily had three siblings and frequently joined them for holidays, birthdays, and other celebrations.

On the basis of individual interviews and psychological tests, they both were rated as healthy young adults. As a couple, Jason and Emily were noted to have many of the characteristics of a healthy marriage. They appeared to have a basic agreement about the structure of their relationship. Both felt that they shared power in decision making, and the research team noted that each participated fully in experimental problem solving. They were interested in each other's opinions and feelings, listened carefully to each other's expressions, and often responded empathically. Although most often they exuded a sense of quiet satisfaction together, there were times when they found much to laugh about.

In separate individual interviews, both Jason and Emily described a satisfactory sexual relationship. They usually made love two or three times a week. Emily was "almost always" orgasmic and said that Jason was an excellent lover. Jason described Emily as a responsive, active participant in their lovemaking.

They looked forward to being parents, with a shared life dream of having "two or three" children, continuing their joint teaching careers, and centering their life on their family.

This quiet, stable, "traditional" couple was rated as having a healthy marriage by the research team. Contrast them with John and Elizabeth.

This couple volunteered for a research project involving families with adolescent children. They were in their mid-40s when first studied. John was a top-level executive in a major real estate firm. Elizabeth's career was in commercial art, but at the time we met them, she was working part-time "because our two teenagers need me to coordinate their wide-ranging activities and to provide transportation."

John and Elizabeth both were seen as having achieved high levels of psychological health. Neither had any lasting anxiety or depression, and, although alcohol was a part of their life, there was no evidence of misuse.

They both seemed to find satisfaction in variety. They were frequent theater-goers, played duplicate bridge together, and liked good wine and fine foods. They had no truly close friends as a couple, but instead saw many casual friends at various social functions.

When observed together, there was something electric about them. They talked rapidly, touched often, and seemed very comfortable when they disagreed about a topic. They interrupted each other's speech, often by finishing the other's sentences.

Each privately described an exciting sexual life. "We make love most nights and try to find new ways to please each other," John related. "Elizabeth is a very passionate gal. Not only about sex, but about everything—food, wine, art, marriage, you name it."

John came from a large Irish Catholic family; Elizabeth's father was an agnostic and her mother was Jewish. Neither believed in God "except as an organizing force in nature," and they did not attend religious services. Although they were devoted to their two sons, it was clear that their relationship with each other was for each the center of life.

Their intense mutual attachment did not interfere with their individual capacities for autonomous functioning. Each had strong opinions, and, although they frequently agreed, when they did not, they seemed to enjoy a respectful debate. "In important matters, we usually compromise," Elizabeth said, "but we seem able to accept our differences, and usually without rancor."

The research team rated theirs as a healthy marriage, noting, in particular, the coexistence of a strong bond and high levels of individual autonomy.

I have selected the Jason–Emily and John–Elizabeth marriages because, despite the partners' very different styles, both marriages were understood as healthy.

ESSENTIAL CHARACTERISTICS OF HEALTHY MARRIAGES

1. Power is shared.

Both partners have participated more or less equally in the definition of the relationship. In part as a consequence of this participation, there is no disagreement about the relationship's basic structure.

2. High levels of both connection and separateness prevail.

There is a strong marital bond characterized by high levels of closeness (much sharing), a strong commitment to the relationship (no outside relationships or activities are more important), and the possibility of psychological intimacy (the reciprocal sharing of vulnerabilities). At the same time, healthy marriages are characterized by high levels of separateness (tolerance for differences), autonomy (the capacity to take care of one's self), and comfortable solitude (the ability to enjoy being alone).

3. There is respect for subjective reality.

The spouses are interested in each other's thoughts and feelings. There is an understanding that what one thinks and feels is a central part of one's world. As a consequence, there is less emphasis on conformity to one spouse's definition of the "truth," and greater emphasis on understanding how each perceives his or her experiences with self and the world. Finding that one's partner's experiences or views may be different from one's own is seen as an opportunity for learning rather than as a threat or an error.

4. The expression of feelings is encouraged.

There are no broad restrictions on the expression either of feelings generally or of particular feelings. Rather, feelings are thought to be a primary aspect of being human, and their appropriate expression is encouraged. Thus, because the participants do not fear the consequences of expressing sadness, joy, anger, selfishness, envy, fear, and other feelings, they learn to know themselves better and to accept the ways in which they are both like and different from others.

The most effective encourager of the expression of feelings is an empathic response. To hear an important other acknowledge your feelings leads to a feeling of being understood, a sense of closer connection with the empathic other, and a deeper exploration of yourself. In healthy marriages, there is a reasonable chance that each spouse will respond empathically to the other.

It is also important that warm, loving feelings be openly expressed. This not only helps each partner maintain self-esteem, but also provides an ambiance that encourages children to give and receive affection. I so often hear from those in couples therapy that one or both partners grew up in a family in which the parents never hugged or said, "I love you."

5. **The inevitable conflicts that do occur do not escalate or lead to despair.**

Life together means inevitable disagreements and, at the very best, occasional conflicts. What, then, is it about disagreement and conflict that separates healthy marriages from dysfunctional ones?

First is a much greater tolerance for differences. There is a greater likelihood that differences are acceptable, or even valuable. Thus, differences less often lead to disagreements and conflicts.

Second is the nature of the disagreements and conflicts that do take place. Because the partners agree about the basic structure of their relationship (the levels of connection and separateness) and tolerate differences, there is no chronic, unresolvable conflict. When disagreements and conflicts arise, they are usually about fairly narrow topics, not about the central nature of the relationship itself. Thus, they are more easily resolved.

Third, disagreements and conflicts are less likely to become generalized and escalate. The partners in healthy relationships are better able to maintain the focus of the conflict through the use of de-escalation maneuvers, such as agreeing to postpone the discussion, interjecting humor, or stepping back to examine what is going on between them. Thus, disagreements are less likely to lead to intense conflicts and conflicts are less likely to lead to painful character attacks.

Finally, the processes of repair are stronger in healthy marriages. In their life together, there will be many occasions on which one partner is not "there" for the other. He or she is thinking about something else, or overlooks something important to the other. Empathic failures are inevitable. When something like this happens, the processes of repair are much more evident in healthy marriages. That is, grudges are short-lived and remorse and forgiveness are common.

6. Problem-solving skills are well developed.

The fact that power is relatively equal and there is respect for each other's subjective reality sets the stage for effective problem solving. Such couples have little, if any, disagreement about the basic structure of their relationship, and thus no underlying conflict poised to erupt with little provocation, which furthers their advantage in problem solving.

Couples with healthy marriages are, therefore, better able to discuss disagreements openly, search for areas of agreement, negotiate compromises, or comfortably agree to disagree.

7. Most basic values are shared.

There is substantial agreement about basic values. Although this similarity of values may be part of what attracts partners to each other initially, living together often means coming to even greater agreement about what is important in life. It is not, as many believe, that certain values characterize healthy marriages, but that partners agree about them.

When the partners disagree about specific values, the disagreement is more apt to be comfortably accepted than to be the focal point of chronic criticism and conflict.

It is clear, for example, that Jason and Emily's basic values are quite different from those of John and Elizabeth. The former couple attaches importance to religious beliefs and practices, security, and the future. The latter partners emphasize the importance of the present, experimentation, and excitement, and believe that life's meaning does not spring from religious beliefs. In both cases, however, the partners agree with each other about these values.

8. The ability to deal with change and stress is well developed.

Change and stress are an inevitable part of life. Children are born and grow up to leave, illnesses become severe or chronic, jobs are threatened or lost. Although we sometimes bring about the stressful circumstances ourselves, quite often bad things just happen. How a couple deals with such experiences can tell us much about their strengths.

There is an increased likelihood that, working together, the partners will deal as effectively as they can with change and stress. They tend to have a greater capacity for anticipating future possibilities and organizing themselves well for action. They do so by getting as many of the facts as possible and, when appropriate, using outside experts for additional input. Their relationship allows them to share their feelings, which can lead to solving problems more effectively. As a result, they are more likely to feel together in facing uncertainty, dealing with losses, and coping with change.

However, there is an important caveat. Severe, chronic stress can overwhelm even the best coping skills. No couple is entirely immune to paying the cost when bad things happen. Even the best relationships can crumble in the worst of circumstances. Nevertheless, it is clear that a healthy marriage provides the strongest, most enduring mechanism for preserving a relationship that gives life meaning.

AN ADMONITION

The characteristics of healthy marriages rarely, if ever, are acquired easily. Their attainment requires hard work that focuses on selflessness, the ability to put the "we" above the "me." This translates into decisions that emphasize the idea of what is best for "us." Thus, decisions about such matters as how time is spent, whether to accept promotions that will result in upheavals in living, or whether to save for the future or spend in the present are framed in terms of the relationship.

SUGGESTIONS

Those who find that their marriages fit this description deserve to feel that, together, they have accomplished something very important. It may be the most creative act of a lifetime, all the more remarkable because it involves the sustained work and ability of two persons.

What, then, is there left to do if you and your spouse have created a healthy marriage? First, you should continue to work on your relationship. Effort is required to maintain a good marriage, so you cannot relax and coast to the finish line. You need to work both on increasing the strength of your marital bond and on becoming even more autonomous. Strengthening your marital bond involves, in particular, two different activities: increasing the closeness by continuing to search for new things to share and enjoy, and increasing the frequency and depth of your intimate conversations. You already have largely overcome the obstacles to this level of communicating, and so your task is mostly to do more of it and to try to get in touch with deeper levels of each other's subjective reality. The question of whether you can have too much closeness and intimacy is largely academic. The key is to have as much as possible, as long as it is balanced by the capacity for autonomy.

Finally, the ability to anticipate the future has been identified as an important individual coping skill. Couples need to anticipate together something of what the future may hold. To illustrate, consider two examples, both of which involve losses. For all but a few, life dreams are never completely realized. Regardless of what stage of life you are in, the ability of a couple to deal jointly with the disappointment about things that haven't quite worked out is an important strength.

Second, there will be real losses in the sense that children will leave, parents will die, and friends will move away, among many others. Dealing with change and loss together can increase the strength of your marital bond.

So, keep talking with each other. Talk, talk, talk.

OTHER TYPES OF MARRIAGES

In both our research and that of others, a small number of types of less healthy marriages have been identified. These marriages fail at one or both of the cardinal tasks of providing an emotional climate that encourages the continued development of the partners, as well as that of their children (the capacities for high levels of *both* connection and separateness).

COMPETENT-BUT-PAINED MARRIAGES

This type of marriage can be considered a "near miss" in that it has many of the features of a healthy marriage, but also involves a disagreement about the basic structure of the relationship. The partners have been unable to negotiate a level of intimacy that is satisfactory to both. One partner wishes for a more intimate relationship in the form of more confiding, a greater focus on inner feelings, and the ability to exchange vulnerabilities. The other partner is content to have a relationship without intimacy. This may be based on unconscious fears of getting close and feeling vulnerable, or on just not knowing how to be intimate as a result of growing up in a family that did not set an example of empathic responses or confiding.

As a consequence of this underlying conflict, one spouse feels deprived, shut out, and lonely. She or he may come to resent the other, but is often caught in the dilemma described by Mary, one of our research volunteers.

> I am so troubled about my relationship with Hal. He's such a *good* man—stable and caring. He's a good provider and a wonderful father. I know he loves me, but he is so remote. He never discusses his inner feelings and isn't interested in mine. If we're not involved with the kids, he's usually in his workshop or watching sports on TV. I feel as though I'm missing something terribly important, a sort of deeper, more meaningful relationship. That's probably why I eat so much. How can I justify to myself the anger I feel toward such a decent man?

That the situation may be somewhat more complex than Mary's anguished comments suggest can be inferred from Hal's comments in a private interview.

> Mary is great mom and she runs the house efficiently. She's not mean, but she's become more and more sour. She's gained a lot of weight and has many physical problems that her doctor can't diagnose. With me, she's sort of bitchy, and some of the time, she's *really* picky. Seems to resent the things I do on my own. With all the good things about her, I find that she's more and more difficult to get close to.

Mary and Hal each sees the other with considerable accuracy, but neither recognizes his or her own role in their joint failure to achieve greater closeness, perhaps even intimacy. Each spouse's subjective reality is invisible to the other.

Despite this important unsolved problem, Mary and Hal show many strengths. They agree on most values, share many interests, and provide good parenting for their children. They can solve outside problems together most of the time. Each functions well as an individual; both provide leadership to various organizations.

Their shared avoidance of intimacy, however, interferes with their free and spontaneous expressions of feelings. It is as if they are fixated at a level of civility: to be too open runs the risk of unearthing their underlying disappointment and the anger each feels toward the other.

Children brought up in this emotional climate often appear to be doing well during childhood and adolescence. How they will function in their adult relationships remains to be seen, but it should be noted that children are very resilient. Less-than-perfect parenting can be "good enough" to produce offspring who become capable and healthy adults.

I would emphasize that neither spouse in this type of marriage draws the children into the underlying conflict. This, along with each spouse's parenting skills, allows the children to develop along healthy lines. Competent-but-pained marriages appear to result in healthy kids, but do not provide the spouses with growth-promoting relationship characteristics.

They do well in nurturing autonomy, but fail to facilitate intimate connection.

SUGGESTIONS

A partner in this type of marriage has much to be grateful for because the marriage has many strengths. But Mary and Hal's statements indicate an underlying problem that needs attention: Mary wants more intimacy than Hal does. Of at least equal importance is the fact that both Mary and Hal are able only to see what the other contributes to the problem, and are unaware of their own contributions. Hal is a solitary man who avoids intimate conversation. Mary is a resentful, picky woman who, despite her wishes, does not invite closeness and intimacy.

How can this type of marriage be improved? The first step is for the partners to stop the blaming and for each to accept 50 percent of the responsibility for the conflict about intimacy. To change such a situation, one must begin by redefining the conflict as a shared problem and accept part of the responsibility instead of focusing only on the partner's contribution. One way to accomplish this is to ask your partner to participate in a joint exercise. Each partner is to write down three changes in the other's behavior that would improve the relationship. These changes should be specific and concrete ("Spend 15 minutes talking with me each day") rather than abstract ("Pay more attention to me"). Each partner must agree to try the other partner's suggestions for at least one week.

The resulting conversations should focus on the suggestions described in Chapter 7. The overall objective is to begin the process of learning more intimate communication and the emphases are to be on empathic processes and facilitating exploration.

If both partners do not make a commitment to the experiment or if there is no progress in the learning process, then they may have to find a couples therapist who is interested in working with them around the issue of intimate communication.

DOMINANT–SUBMISSIVE MARRIAGES

This type of marriage probably has been the most common throughout history. It has only been in fairly recent times that patriarchy has waned, at least in some parts of the world.

Therapists see both male- and female-dominated marriages. Often the partners come for help when the less powerful spouse develops such symptoms as depression or a drinking problem. Sometimes a couple will come for help with a disturbed child, who often proves to be the submissive spouse's unconscious confederate in opposing the dominant spouse's controllingness. Many others come because of increasing conflict; the dominant–submissive structure has become unsatisfactory to one partner.

A sizable number of the volunteer couples who were in unequal relationships of this kind said they believed that they had healthy relationships. What makes the difference between those who feel good about themselves and those who are troubled?

Several factors are involved, one of which is the extent of the dominant partner's power. If he or she is much more powerful (and therefore very controlling), the other spouse may eventually resent his or her childlike status. In couples with less of a power differential, the more powerful spouse may take into consideration the wishes of his or her partner, and tolerate some degree of autonomy in the less powerful spouse.

A second factor relates to how much the less powerful spouse enjoys not having too many adult responsibilities. If being taken care of is agreeable to the submissive spouse, the relationship may be satisfactory to both. If, on the other hand, the submissive spouse comes to resent her or his powerlessness, conflict will ensue. The less powerful spouse may then use passive–aggressive retaliation (e.g., forgetting to record checks or being chronically late) or will develop an oppositional alliance with a child, friend, lover, or parent. Finally, some spouses in this situation develop depression or become dependent on alcohol or drugs, which can be understood, in part, as reflecting their marital unhappiness, as well as an attempt to become more powerful. Here is what a depressed, alcoholic woman told me.

Chuck is a real controller. He micromanages every aspect of our life—I'm still on the allowance he gave me 15 years ago.

He makes all the decisions. I end up angry much of the time. The only things he *can't* control are my drinking and pills and depression, and that drives him wild. That's not *why* I'm depressed and drinking, of course, but I guess I do get some secret satisfaction out of seeing him feel as helpless as I have felt for all these years.

Some religious and ethnic traditions support dominant–submissive relationships in which the husband is the dominant spouse. Unfortunately, however, dominant–submissive marriages do not encourage the continued development of the spouses, and may leave the children lacking in the skills needed for both intimacy and autonomy. Feelings often must be hidden, true negotiation is impossible, and a locked-in rigidity may limit all family members.

Problems with power lead to divorce more often than does falling out of love, according to some marriage researchers. When the dominant spouse grows tired of having all the responsibility or the submissive spouse tires of powerlessness, conflict may follow, with the dissolution of the relationship.

Dominant–submissive marriages fail to allow the dominant partner to learn the skills of closeness and intimacy, while preventing the submissive partner from becoming comfortably autonomous. Children in such families may develop a distorted view of how marriage "should" work, and, as adults, often have problems of their own with intimacy, autonomy, or both.

Suggestions

Although dominant–submissive relationships sometimes are satisfactory to both spouses, they fail to encourage the continued development of the partners. They also may provide an overly rigid environment for the children, and in male-dominated marriages, may model restricted gender roles.

Many partners find this type of marriage unsatisfactory, with the less powerful spouse becoming dissatisfied with her or his "one down" position and asking for more equality.

From an optimistic viewpoint, however, consider that many such relationships are seen as gradually becoming less dominant–submissive as the partners move into the middle and later stages of life. This view is supported by studies of adult development that report that men (usually more dominant) are said to tend to mellow as time goes on, and women (usually less powerful) to become more assertive.

On the other hand, a more pessimistic outlook suggests that no change is possible unless the more powerful partner is willing to give up some of his or her power. Since most clinicians believe that a common dynamic underlying the need for power is fear (of closeness, abandonment, or other, usually unconscious themes), the key issue is to deal with the fear in order to reduce the controlling behavior.

This idea is the focus of my treatment efforts with such couples. It explains why the common and understandable reactions of the unhappy submissive spouse do not usually have an effect. To respond with passive–aggressive tactics (e.g., for-

getfulness, lateness, or inefficiency) often *increases* the dominant spouse's underlying fear and justifies his or her
controllingness, as is also true of tactics of embarrassment (such
as drinking too much or acting inappropriately in public). The
same mechanism frequently operates when the submissive
spouse adopts (usually not deliberately) the sick role. The point
is that these understandable responses to frustration over the
lack of power tend to backfire: they increase that which they
are designed to decrease (the dominant spouse's need to control).

What can the less powerful spouse do? First, she or he must
try to give up the ineffective mechanisms I have described. Second, the submissive spouse must understand that there may be
golden moments in which the process of change is enhanced.
Such moments are usually inspired by some crisis in the life of
the dominant spouse, which may be work related (loss of job,
failure to get a promotion), family related (death of a parent),
or personal (contracting a serious illness).

In all of these circumstances, the dominant spouse's underlying fears become accessible. If the less powerful spouse is
able to help his or her partner explore these fears, an experience of closeness, even intimacy, may result. However, it generally takes more than one such experience to reduce the
dominant spouse's fears of not being in control.

The key to this type of change is to help the dominant spouse
to develop an increased capacity for intimacy.

If it is the dominant spouse who wishes the change, it is often
because he or she feels increasingly overwhelmed by the re-

sponsibility engendered by his or her controllingness. In that case, the less powerful spouse's ability to function autonomously must be encouraged. Chapter 8 outlines my suggestions for the kinds of conversations that can help in this process.

Under the best of circumstances, if both spouses agree that a change is desirable, each helps the other. The goals are for the dominant spouse to give up some or all of his or her control of the relationship while learning greater intimacy, and for the less powerful spouse to give up some or all of his or her submissiveness (or ineffectual responses) while learning to function with greater autonomy.

Many couples in dominant–submissive relationships either cannot or will not change their unequal partnerships. They require the help of a therapist, preferably a couples therapist who can focus on the ways in which each partner contributes to the dominant–submissive structure.

Finally, what can one do if the spouse refuses either to acknowledge the problem, to try to change the relationship, or to seek help? I assist people in exploring their options, but the decisions must come from them because they are the ones who must live with the consequences. Still, there are some marriages in which the dominant–submissive structure is so rigid, the emotional climate so cold, and the effects on their health so negative that I wonder what could possibly make it worthwhile for two people to remain locked in such a disastrous relationship.

Most couples in a dominant–submissive relationship, however, can change. By either working on change themselves or seeking professional help, their rigid, overly controlled, distant relationship can improve. One partner can learn to fear intimacy less and the other to be less afraid of autonomy.

CONFLICTED MARRIAGES

Some years ago, I read an account of a psychologist's interviews with a number of couples on their 50th wedding anniversaries. Although many of those couples reported positively about their half-centuries together, a surprising minority said that it had been 50 years of pure hell. One 75-year-old man described his 50-year marriage as follows:

> Every day has been miserable. Our getting married was the worst mistake of our lives. We argue all the time. Haven't said "I love you" in years. No hugging or kissing, and there's been no sex since our last child was born 40 years ago. I wonder why we stayed together. Part of it was my work. A divorced minister might lose his pulpit and she probably felt she was incapable of supporting herself. Whatever the case, it's been a terrible relationship.

This tragic narrative poses a painful question. What is the real or underlying reason that people with chronically conflicted marriages often stay together, even in these days of easy divorce? I struggled with the answer to this question for years until, finally, several couples I treated began to open my eyes. They taught me that chronic conflict has a purpose: it keeps people who have intense underlying fears both of closeness and of being alone from getting too close or being too lonely. Anger and conflict keep the partners involved, but at a comfortable distance.

Couples stay in conflicted marriages because they are afraid of closeness, afraid of the vulnerability that is involved. Such couples almost always report childhood experiences that make their avoidance of closeness understandable. Rejection, neglect, abandonment, and abuse lead to fears of closeness. And yet, we all need someone, if for no other reason than being totally alone is the ultimate dread. This combination of intense fear and deep need can lead many into conflicted relationships and keep them unhappily (but safely) connected for a lifetime.

It is evident, nevertheless, that chronic conflict has many harmful effects on the partners and on their children. For one, there is the increased likelihood that they will become depressives or substance abusers. Recent studies also have shown deleterious effects on blood pressure and the immune system. Children growing up in the climate of ongoing parental conflict may show physical symptoms by the age of four. Thus, the price of this tenuous balance of fear and need is very high for all family members.

There are two types of chronically conflicted relationships. One involves more or less constant conflict, sullenness, tension, and anger that often erupt in vicious attacks. In the second type, a period of quiet civility, perhaps even real pleasure, is followed by a period of conflict that results in pushing the partners apart. The relationship then moves back to another period of calm, only to be interrupted by another period of conflict and distance.

These two patterns (constant and intermittent) are understood to be based on similar dynamics of fear of closeness and intimacy in both partners. Both partners may be capable of independence and autonomy, but this type of marriage neither facilitates the growth of the partners nor encourages the healthy development of the children. Although an intermittently conflicted marriage may have fewer harmful effects than an environment of constant conflict, few survive either type unscathed.

SUGGESTIONS

Partners who are caught up in a pattern of constant conflict may need a skilled psychotherapist, and sooner rather than later. Chronic, always-present conflict is so harmful—emotionally and physically—both to the spouses and to their children that the welfare of all can be dramatically improved by a shared spousal commitment to seek help. Also, it may not be possible for constantly warring partners to follow the suggestions or to engage in the exercises offered in Chapters 7 and 8. As with dominant–submissive partners, however, familiarity with the concepts described may improve the prognosis and speed the progress of psychotherapeutic intervention.

If the pattern of conflict is intermittent, there is a greater likelihood that the couple can do something about it on their own, because their underlying fears are less intense. They "allow" for periods of civility, and even some closeness. Another factor is that the contrast between the calm periods and the conflicted periods is so strong that one or both partners may ask what is going on. This is particularly true if the pattern of calm–conflict–calm is recognized by both, as in the following example.

"There's something wrong with our relationship," the woman said. "We get along well, usually for several months, and then something happens. We're at each other's throats, and it's usually over some little, insignificant disagreement."

"It's like we can't stand getting along well for too long," her husband added.

Although this couple did not have an intimate relationship, they did have considerable closeness (sharing), and it was these periods that ended in conflict and distance.

In my therapy, such couples generally have a good prognosis. The intensity of their blaming each other is low in contrast to the constant-conflict pattern, where it usually is high. The couple described above did little blaming (except at the peak of their conflict periods) and were ready to look at their interactions unhampered by a sense of being the victim.

In couples therapy, it is often possible to help them discover that, immediately prior to the conflict, they had enjoyed a time (minutes, hours, or days) of unusually intense closeness. It is as if this closeness stirred up their underlying fears and they unconsciously created a conflict in order to retreat to a period of safety brought about by the distance the conflict produces.

The critical issues in couples therapy are, first, to help both

partners get in touch with their underlying fears and each partner to become aware of the other's fears. The second task is to
encourage sharing the fears rather than being defensive and
angry. To the extent that both partners become aware of their
underlying vulnerabilities and can begin to share them, the conflicts can be averted.

It is important to recognize that disagreements and conflict
are inevitable. Thus, the key to improvement is early repair and
breaking the pattern of conflict and distance. Since the basic
dynamic in these couples is a shared fear of too much closeness, the suggestions in Chapter 7 regarding learning how to
be intimate (and, therefore, vulnerable) should help. If the partners, working together, cannot change the pattern, seeing a
couples therapist will often assist them to do so.

SEVERELY DYSFUNCTIONAL MARRIAGES

Some marriages can be understood as even more disturbed
than the chronically conflicted type. Two such severely dysfunctional patterns of marriage are the *alienated* and the *fused*.

Some people live out their lives in a state of extreme distance
from others; they have no significant emotional contacts. When
they do marry, it is usually to someone like themselves and for
reasons of convenience ("two can live more cheaply than
one"), obligation ("I owe it to my parents to get married"), or
religious beliefs ("God tells us to marry").

The resulting *alienated* marriages are characterized by very
high levels of separateness with no true connectedness. These

marriages do nothing to promote the personality growth of either partner.

The underlying dynamics may be complex. There may be an inherited, neurological, or pervasive developmental disability. Some alienated individuals have been severely abused and are terrified of any closeness. Others have grown up in alienated families. A young physician came to see me after a series of love affairs, each of which was terminated by the man. She reported:

> My parents had a very strange relationship. They slept in different rooms and lived mostly separate lives. They were civil to each other, but there was no open affection. Most of the time, they were occupied with individual interests. They had different friends, and no couple friends. They never fought and hardly ever seemed to disagree. They just seemed not at all connected.

Another type of severely dysfunctional marriage can be thought of as *fused*. In some ways, it is the opposite of the alienated marriage. In the fused marriage, there is no "I," only a "we." All efforts at self-determination are disallowed, all differences are blurred, and often there is an operating metaphor of "us against the world."

Therapists tend to see the partners in such marriages as seriously flawed. Their sense of self has not been completely developed and they desperately need another person to give them any feeling of completeness.

A medical school classmate entered into a fused relationship with his wife-to-be, and they quickly became uncomfortable to be around. They attended only to each other, and it was as if they had constructed a high wall around their relationship. They began to dress alike and to speak in the plural: "We think" and "We feel." They seemed happy together, but had trouble raising healthy children. Any separation from each other was very disturbing, and when the man became seriously ill and was put in intensive care, his wife became floridly psychotic.

This vignette speaks to the twin difficulties of such fused marriages. Parenting is usually deficient and separations are intolerable. To be separated from one's spouse may be equated psychologically with death of the self.

It seems clear that fused marriages emphasize connection without separateness and that alienated marriages emphasize separateness without connection. Neither is good for your health, or for that of your children.

We know relatively little about the internal life of spouses in severely dysfunctional marriages. There are several reasons for this, not the least of which is that such unions apparently are not common. Second, the adults in severely dysfunctional marriages seldom come to psychotherapists, and tend to terminate contact quickly when they do. Third, alienated and fused couples alike tend to avoid volunteering for (or quickly drop out of) research studies. Suspiciousness and distrust of strangers, along with deeply ingrained needs for distance from neighbors, coworkers, and professionals, are characteristic of the loners in these unusual marriages. As a result, my suggestions should be taken as tentative at best.

SUGGESTIONS

Partners in a fused marriage have a shared problem with separateness, autonomy, self-sufficiency, and comfort in being alone. I suspect that they are unlikely, however, to seek either self-help or psychotherapy until one dies or becomes disabled, leaving the other bereft. At that point, the shaken survivor may become available to support from—and, therefore, a chance for an improved relationship with—a relative, neighbor, religious counselor, helpful physician, or psychotherapist. If personal growth begins to take place, additional healing may become possible. The material in Chapter 8 may be especially helpful.

Spouses in alienated marriages have a shared deficit in the skills of intimacy and closeness, and are unlikely to be willing to risk working to overcome these deficits unless life circumstances (a major loss or change) upset the balance of needs and fears underlying their preference for autonomy without closeness. Even a very small narrowing of the gap between the partners, using whichever techniques in Chapter 7 are most comfortable, may bring about a substantial improvement in one's feelings of being valued by one's spouse (and children), relief from feelings of anxiety or depression that may have resulted from the disruptive change or loss, and a newfound sense of meaning in life.

REMEMBER . . .

Maintaining a marriage that is good for both spouses and for their children is not easy. It can be done, however, and our research volunteers have taught us much about what to work for and what to watch out for.

It is encouraging to note that while marital patterns are more or less stable, they are not fixed. Just as chronic severe stress can lower the quality of marital life, so can that quality be *improved* by working hard on learning the skills one needs to function better.

~∾~

chapter seven

Learning How To Be Intimate

There are things a person can learn alone, but intimacy is not one of them. It takes two persons to create a period of intimacy; indeed, it is a characteristic of a relationship, not something an individual either has or does not have.

Intimacy may be defined as the reciprocal sharing of vulnerabilities, the ability both to tell an important other something very private and to listen carefully to the private revelations of the other.

As explained previously, three major factors determine an individual's capacity for connecting to an important other: intimacy, commitment, and closeness. Both commitment and closeness are understood to increase the likelihood that intimacy may develop, but they do not ensure it. Many couples capable of commitment and closeness go through life having never experienced a moment of intimacy.

You can have a satisfactory and effective relationship without intimacy, but its presence almost always is a marker of one that is highly competent and mutually satisfying. Spouses who have achieved an intimate level of relating usually mention that fact first when asked to describe what is important in their marriage.

A person's capacity to enter into an intimate relationship is created by the interplay of four major factors: inherited brain wiring, early childhood experiences with the primary caretaker, family "rules" about what is permissible to share with others, and the presence or absence of underlying, usually unconscious, fears that intimacy will lead to being hurt.

It appears that our inborn brain wiring makes learning the skills of intimate communication much easier for some than for others. It also appears that inborn deficits in these skills can be overcome to some degree by favorable life experiences. A primary caretaker who is very sensitive to the moment-to-moment feelings and needs of the infant aids the developing child's capacity to be in touch with his or her own feelings and to be sensitive to the feelings of others.

With regard to the importance of power in establishing the basic structure of a relationship, one of the significant findings from our research at the Timberlawn Research Foundation was that when couples share power more or less equally, there is a greater possibility that intimacy will develop. Intimacy is rarely seen in relationships based on clearly unequal assignments of power since one cannot demand or impose intimacy— it takes two willing partners. In chronically conflicted relationships, intimacy is experienced as too dangerous ("If you knew how I felt, you would use it against me").

Equal or shared power means, among other things, that your thoughts, feelings, and beliefs are of equal importance as those of your partner, and that his or her wants and needs are as important as yours. This mutual respect makes it safe to explore and share private thoughts, feelings, or experiences that could lead to being embarrassed, or even humiliated, by a less respectful or more judgmental listener. Such deep sharing is too risky if your partner has more power over you than you have over him or her (dominates you), or if you are battling for control (chronically conflicted). Spouses with equal power feel safer talking about fears, failures, inadequacies, or conventionally disapproved-of material (greed, envy, vengeful impulses, indiscretions, misjudgments), knowing that these "shameful" admissions will be accepted by the important other without a negative value judgment. This, in turn, increases each spouse's respect for the subjective reality of the other.

The aspect of intimate sharing that bonds partners more and more closely is the feeling of being deeply understood. The power of deep understanding—being fully known with no deceptions, no omissions, and no loss of love or dignity—cannot be exaggerated. The infant with a loving, consistent, and understanding caretaker; the psychotherapy patient with a warm, genuine, and deeply empathic therapist; and the spouse in an intimate relationship come to know their own feelings and needs more fully as their respect for, and healthy attachment to, the empathic other grows.

This, of course, is the foundation of what we call *self-esteem*: a realistic perception of one's own basic worth, value, and lovability that develops gradually over time through a close connection to a warm, respectful, empathic, and nurturing other. This also explains the foreordained failure of misguided attempts to raise children's self-esteem solely by phoney praise, undeserved "success experiences," and trivial ribbons and awards.

When a couple is able to have discussions in which private hopes, feelings, fears, dreams, wishes, and actions can be discussed openly and honestly, at least three other benefits are fostered.

First, research has shown that an intimate, confiding relationship buffers against the development of certain psychiatric disorders (depression, for example), reduces the severity of the disorders that do occur, and greatly increases resistance to relapse once recovery has taken place.

Second, stable intimate relationships have been shown to improve the parenting skills of previously abused or neglected spouses, thereby making it possible to stop the damage from being passed down from generation to generation.

Third, there even are physiological consequences: studies have demonstrated that our immune systems are impaired by conflict and enhanced by confiding.

EMPATHY

The royal road to an enhanced capacity for intimacy is empathy. Unlike intimacy, empathy is an individual characteristic. It is the ability to recognize the feelings of another and to let the other know that he or she is understood. Thus, at its core, empathy means *sensitivity to feelings.*

Any communication to an important other consists of three parts—the content or information, the feeling, and the relationship component. The last can be very subtle, and involves how the speaker would like the listener to respond. The truly empathic person usually hears all three components, but the most important is sensitivity to feelings. This is so because marital communication (indeed, all communication) takes place at levels ranging from superficial to deep. Normal greetings ("Hi, nice to see you") and other stereotyped interchanges occupy the most *superficial level* of communication. Words and phrases are exchanged in a fairly meaningless fashion, much the same whether with friends or enemies.

Bland, businesslike communications about largely noncontroversial facts, feelings, and other issues make up the *casual level.* Casual conversation is designed to allow us to get to know each other without risking too much ("I enjoyed the movie—how about you?"), or to accomplish goal-directed tasks ("I'll get the car gassed and washed if you'll pack the lunch, and then we can leave for the lake"). Both superficial and casual conversations are focused on content, are relatively devoid of feelings, and are expected to be clear and direct about the *relationship or intention* component. (When I say, "It's nice to see you," you are supposed to respond in kind; when I say, "I enjoyed the movie," you're supposed to agree, or else be very polite and tactful in your disagreement. "I'll get the car ready if you'll fix the food" is quite clear and direct about intention.)

The next level, where we begin to share potentially controversial ideas or feelings, the *personal level,* involves much greater risk. Discussions about politics, religion, sexual preferences, racial or ethnic attitudes, gender bias, and similar topics reveal our personal ideas or feelings and expose us to acceptance, judgment, or rejection by the listener, openly or secretly. Small children often say whatever comes to mind ("Daddy, why is Grandma so fat?"); this can be embarrassing, and sometimes hurtful, so we teach them to suppress their personal observations and develop keen judgment about when, where, and with whom to share at this level.

A crucial part of the unconscious negotiation of a new relationship involves sharing increasingly personal material, "testing" the other to see how well he or she understands and how genuinely he or she accepts your subjective reality.

It is at this personal level that one's skills (or lack of skills) in accurately "reading" the content, feelings, and intentions implicit in the partner's communications begin to lead to greater closeness—or to drive a wedge between you. The listener's accurate understanding and nonjudgmental acceptance of the feeling component of personal communications sends a powerful message of respect, safety, and trustworthiness to the speaker. Misunderstandings or disagreements concerning the content or the speaker's intentions are relatively painless and easily negotiated, whereas "missing the point" about personal feelings more often sends a signal of disrespect (whether intended or not). If you say you are terribly frightened about some task or issue and the listener responds, "That's nothing to be afraid of," you have just been told, in effect, that you are being irrational and childish—a message not likely to make you feel deeply understood or highly valued.

Accurate empathic sensitivity for the feeling component of communications is even more important at the deepest level— that of *intimate sharing.* This level involves talking about feelings, hopes, wishes, dreams, and experiences that one would share only with a reliably trustworthy, supportive, benevolent partner. The crucial aspect of such communications is that the material offered is so private that the speaker becomes very vulnerable to every nuance of the listener's response. Any hint of negative judgment, lack of interest, ridicule, or giving advice turns an opportunity for intense closeness into a painful encounter that discourages further intimacy.

Attentive, accurate, nonjudgmental reflection of the speaker's feelings, however, signals connection at the intimate level of communication, and brings such intense feelings of closeness and acceptance that both partners are encouraged to share more vulnerability-laden material in the future.

For over 30 years, I have been teaching beginning therapists to be sensitive to feelings. During that time, I have experimented with various techniques, many of which also have proved effective in couples therapy. The two basic elements of the techniques are enhanced listening and reflective responding.

To develop a better ear for feelings, it is helpful either to have a partner to practice with or to use a tape recorder. If a tape recorder is employed, have a partner or friend record a series of statements, each involving the expression of a particular feeling, such as:

"I'm concerned about the test tomorrow."

"I'm so pleased that she's coming home."

"I'm angry about what he did."

"I feel so sad when I think about it."

"I'm ashamed when I think of what I did."

"I worry a lot about the future."

The first step is to *listen for the feeling word*. In the foregoing examples, these words are *concerned, pleased, angry, sad, ashamed*, and *worry*. It only takes a little practice to listen selectively for such feeling words.

An equally important exercise is to develop enhanced sensitivity to feelings that are not openly labeled by the speaker. Have someone say or record another series of statements in which the speaker expresses feelings but does not label them. Examples might be:

"I've got that test tomorrow." (Said with apprehension)

"She's coming home!" (Said with excitement)

"I can't believe what he did." (Said angrily)

"It's hard to think about." (Said sadly)

"I can't believe I did it." (Said with chagrin)

These expressions of feelings are more difficult to identify accurately because, rather than being labeled by the speaker, they are expressed by more subtle cues. The better one knows the speaker, the greater is the likelihood that the specific feeling can be identified, but there is a helpful rule.

When responding to the speaker's feelings, use the same feeling word that the speaker used. If the speaker does not label his or her feelings, but communicates them through more subtle cues, use a general rather than a specific descriptor of feelings. To illustrate both types of responses:

"I'm *concerned* about the test tomorrow."

"It is something to be *concerned* about."

"I'm so *pleased* that she's coming home."

"It's very *pleasing.*"

If the feelings are not directly described, the use of general descriptors can take the following form.

"I've got that test tomorrow."

"It is upsetting."

"She's coming home!"

"It's exciting."

Responses to feeling messages that are not specifically labeled use general descriptors, such as *upsetting, painful, wonderful, distressing, bothersome, hurt, alarming, worrisome, exciting.* Using such general descriptors acknowledges that feelings are being expressed, but that the specific feeling has yet to be labeled.

Notice that in the above examples the emphasis is on the phrase, "It is _____." Many persons find it more natural to say, "You are upset" (or excited, worried, sad, angry). Although that is acceptable empathic language, the "It is _____." has the advantage of suggesting that the listener can actually put himself or herself inside the speaker's feelings.

The idea of being inside the feelings of an important other

rather than only understanding that which the other is feeling brings up different levels of empathy. Recognizing and letting the other know you have recognized his or her feelings can be thought of as baseline empathy. A deeper level of empathy involves actually feeling that which the other is feeling. Thus, if the listener actually feels sad upon hearing the other say, "I feel so sad when I think about it," a deeper level of empathy has been achieved. The two persons are *sharing the experience of the feeling*, and often, as a result, feel very close to each other.

We all start by learning baseline empathy. As with most learning, repetition is important. For some, developing an ear for feelings comes easily, but for most of us, it takes considerable practice.

Although the most important result of empathy is that it leads to feeling understood, another clear benefit is that it often results in further discussion. Empathic responses can lead the speaker to more and deeper self-exploration—and this is why accurate empathic responding is the hallmark of the well-trained psychotherapist.

EXPLORATORY CONVERSATIONS

Many partners never learn to help each other explore a thought, feeling, or experience. They don't listen attentively, or they change the subject, ask focused questions, offer advice, or pass judgment. All of these responses shut down exploration; they take the speaker away from exploring his or her own experience. There are times, of course, when one wants advice or judgment, but when sharing one's most private self with a spouse, what one most often wants and needs is to be listened to and helped to understand better what is on one's mind.

Exploratory conversations involve the efforts of the listener to help the speaker come to a richer understanding of his or her own experiences. Such conversations are based on the idea of subjective reality—the unique way one feels or thinks about or understands a particular experience. The term emphasizes that each individual has his or her own unique way of experiencing; no two persons are affected by a particular situation in exactly the same way.

Further, in relationships, a person's subjective reality is usually far more important than is objective "truth," whatever that may be. Relationships are much more satisfactory to both participants if each respects the other's subjective reality. Couples who come to me for help are often arguing about the truth. "No, that's not what happened. What *really* happened is. . . ." I tell such couples that the truth is important if their car is stalled on the railroad tracks since they must know whether or not a train is coming. More often, however, to listen to and show respect for each other's way of seeing things (no matter how different it may be from one's own way) is more important.

In exploratory conversations, one attempts to attain as complete an understanding of another's subjective reality as possible. Often the conversation also results in the storyteller's attaining a better understanding of his or her own subjective reality. Thus, exploratory conversations may lead to increased understanding for both participants. To arrive at a new understanding of the subjective reality of one or both participants (the co-creating of new meanings) often also creates a shared sense of intense closeness.

To have a successful exploratory conversation, one must encourage the other to continue to explore his or her experience with as little interference as possible. The major encouragers of exploration are empathic statements. The most powerful way to encourage another to continue exploring his or her subjective reality is to demonstrate an accurate understanding of the feelings that are being expressed.

Another way to facilitate self-exploration is to use general encouragers. "Tell me more," "Go on," "What else does that bring to mind?" "How interesting," and similar statements *encourage the storyteller to continue, but without suggesting the direction the story should take.* In exploratory conversations, we want the story to unfold from inside the storyteller, rather than to be shaped or directed by the questions or comments of the listener.

For example, when cross-examining a witness, a lawyer is very active, asking one pointed question after another, frequently focusing on "who, what, where, or when." In this way, the lawyer determines where the interview is going, and, in that sense, it is a *directive* (not an exploratory) inquiry.

In exploratory conversations, any sense of cross-examination is to be avoided. The listener must put out of mind any conviction about the direction of the discussion or where it should end. For this reason, there is always a sense of adventure about exploratory conversations.

Are questions ever called for in exploratory conversations? Of course, particularly if they open up possibilities rather than narrow them. If, for example, a person says, "I always get nervous when I have to speak to a group," an opening-up question might be, "Are there times when you are more nervous or less nervous than usual when speaking to a group?" This question does not direct the storyteller away from his or her experience, but requests a closer examination.

On the other hand, to respond with the question, "When did that start?" *directs* the speaker to look for the "cause"—a listener-imposed change of direction. Even more disruptive of the exploration process, and more difficult to avoid, is a "helpful" or reassuring response: "No one who knows as much as you do about the topic should ever be nervous about presenting it, and besides, you're a great public speaker." Many of us were raised on such supposedly helpful comments from our parents, and we find ourselves repeating them without thinking, believing that this is how we are supposed to respond. Unfortunately, responses of "You don't really feel that way" or "Stop being childish" signal the speaker that you are rejecting his or her subjective reality and that you wish the person to share your denial of this experience. Variations of this response of "Don't feel that way" are one of the most common causes of the lack of intimacy in marriage.

Another way to encourage self-exploration is through check-out summaries. "Let me see if I understand," followed by a brief summary of what one has heard, does several things: it reassures the storyteller that you are really listening, it invites further elaboration, and it encourages the speaker to correct or modify the description of his or her subjective reality.

Here is a brief segment of an exploratory conversation.

> "Mary didn't show up for our lunch today. It really bothered me."
>
> "Yeah, that is bothersome."
>
> "Well, it's not the first time it's happened."
>
> "That makes it hurt even more."
>
> "It really does. I begin to wonder if I'm really important to her."
>
> "How could you not at least wonder?"
>
> "Well, you know I'm very sensitive to any hint of rejection."
>
> "Yes, you've talked about that from time to time. It's hard for any of us to feel rejected, but you've thought it was an especially sensitive area for you."
>
> "Well, yes. You know that I never felt that Mom valued me like she did my brother. He was her favorite."
>
> "And that's kind of where it all started?"
>
> "I think so. [Thoughtful pause] You know, Mary could have messed up on the date of our lunch or any number of things. But for me, it revives that old feeling—it's easy to jump to the conclusion that she doesn't care."
>
> "I know it is, but here, as you talk about it, you seem to be trying to put it into a broader perspective."

Although this conversation took only a minute, it was an important relationship-enhancing experience. If such exploratory conversations take place from time to time (and in a reciprocal manner), they are likely to foster very strong and deep feelings of closeness. It is important to emphasize what the listener did to make the exploration possible. The listener:

1. Was truly attentive.

2. Showed respect for the partner's subjective reality.

3. Responded with empathic statements.

4. Did *not* change the subject, downplay or disagree with the speaker's concern, offer advice, or pass judgment.

As a result, the partner either made or reaffirmed important connections between a present experience and a very personal and private sensitivity based on early experiences.

CRUCIAL REPAIRS

I have suggested that partners may truly connect with each other on fewer than half of the occasions that a close connection is sought by one of them. At such times, the other partner is unavailable emotionally, usually because he or she is too tired, preoccupied, or anxious. If, however, one's partner is *never* available for connecting conversations, it may be safe to assume that he or she either doesn't know how to connect closely with an important other or is unconsciously afraid that the resulting closeness will lead to being hurt (abandoned, rejected, attacked, controlled, or devalued in some way). Often such consistently unavailable partners need the help of a therapist to overcome the block.

Most spouses, however, have some capacity for connecting through empathy, exploration, and respect for subjective reality. But even truly sensitive partners probably miss more often than they connect. This makes the process of repair a crucial factor in learning intimacy in a relationship.

The spouse seeking the connection needs to be certain that he or she has been clear that what is wanted is to be heard and understood, not to be given advice or judged. If the partner does not respond as one wishes, it is important not to become upset or angry. Explore the circumstances: "Is this not a good time for us to talk?" or, "I need you to listen to what I'm hung up on—when would it be best to try?"

The responding spouse must be clear if the problem is that there is something on his or her mind that is interfering with careful listening. "I'm sorry, I'm still at the office," or, "I'm preoccupied myself—let's try to talk after dinner." Suggesting another time is very helpful, both at a practical level and as a sign of respect for the partner's concerns.

Even if the repair does not occur at the time, the partner who was not available can help the situation later by expressing *remorse*. "I'm sorry I wasn't there for you earlier today. I'll try to do better next time," can make a big difference. In a similar vein, the disappointed spouse can express *gratitude* for the times the partner was available, thus assisting the repair process.

It should be emphasized that being disappointed when a loved one fails to connect with one's inner experience is inevitable in even the best of relationships. The important issue is the type of response pattern the couple establishes. For many, these periods of dysynchrony always lead to conflict, whereas for others, the pattern is that of repair. *The repair pattern is a prominent characteristic of couples who find healing in their relationship.*

In couples therapy, there is a very helpful technique to assist a couple in learning repair processes. Most often, the couple reports a conflict that took place between sessions. I ask them to replay the conversation in my office, and I interrupt them whenever either partner shows irritation or open anger with the other. I ask them to focus internally on what feeling preceded the anger. Almost always, they report a hurt or fear, which is quickly converted (usually unconsciously) to anger. I next ask the couple to redo the conversation, only this time *expressing the hurt or fear rather than the anger.* When they do so, they usually initiate the repair process. The other spouse almost always responds helpfully and does not defend himself or herself, as is usual when one is the target of an important other's anger.

I ask them to use this technique between sessions, and indicate that, although initially they'll probably continue to fail and move on to a conflict situation, they can, with repetition, learn the repair process. If this doesn't happen, I need to explore with them why they are not able to change from the conflict pattern to the repair pattern. "You both do it well here in my office, but you don't ever seem to manage it at home. What do you make of that?" Such responses usually lead us to a beginning understanding of their resistances. Most often, these resistances are based on their fears of the wished-for intimacy.

I suggest that readers practice this approach. Remember, the secret is to identify the fear or hurt that is usually behind the anger. Tell your spouse about the fear or hurt rather than lashing out. Watch the response: there is a good chance it will be one that repairs.

LEARNING INTIMACY

If they are to have any chance of learning to be more intimate, couples must commit time and effort to the endeavor. This is important because one partner often is more motivated than the other to change the relationship. The less enthusiastic partner must make the necessary commitment and live up to it; intimacy cannot be learned on one's own.

One concrete measure of both partners' commitment is their agreeing on a time to carry out the exercises described below. At that time, neither spouse should be tired, preoccupied with other matters, or angry. Child care, telephone calls, and similar practical issues must be delegated to someone else or postponed because the exercises require a high level of attention.

Also essential is a recording device. A few couples prefer to use a video recorder, which has the advantage of their being able to review nonverbal messages. A good tape recorder is satisfactory, however, if the discussions can be heard clearly.

Hearing one's self can have a profound impact. Many persons have said to me something like, "I can't believe I sound so defensive (or angry, uninterested, or unemotional)." Another frequent observation is the tendency to repeat the same "mistake" over and over again. "I can't believe that I continue to ask such pointed questions and express so much of my opinion. I wonder why I can't stop doing something I know is counterproductive." This vital piece of learning would not be available without a recording to review.

The exercises are discussion tasks that introduce the partners to the key ideas of subjective reality, exploratory conversations, and empathic responsiveness. Here are the basic instructions.

Once you practice with your tape recorder to be sure your normal speaking voice can be clearly heard, I want you to experiment with a particular type of conversation, called an *exploratory conversation*. I want one of you to describe an occasion on which you felt vulnerable in the sense of feeling afraid or alone, or having some other unpleasant feeling. The experience could have taken place yesterday or years ago when you were a child. The vulnerability experience should not, however, have involved the partner. If at all possible, I'd like it to be an experience that you have not previously shared with your partner.

The listener has the more complex job. You are to respond

in ways that encourage the speaker to further explore the experience of vulnerability and, at the same time, lead to the speaker's concluding that you are truly interested and trying to understand.

I select an experience of vulnerability for several reasons. First, intimacy is defined as the exchange of vulnerabilities. It is as accurate a sign as any that a relationship involves high levels of mutual satisfaction. Thus, it makes sense to try to begin the process of talking about vulnerabilities as quickly as possible. Second, recollections of experiences of vulnerabilities often shed light on important underlying life themes that have not been fully recognized. Finally, allowing your partner to know something of your vulnerabilities may well result in your partner's coming to a new and deeper understanding of you.

After one has tried to help the other to explore such an experience, change roles. The former speaker now becomes the listener, and vice versa. Although how long each exploration takes to accomplish can vary considerably, usually they last from 5 to 20 minutes.

Among other topics that often result in much mutual learning are early memories and hopes for the future. But for most couples, reciprocal exploration of three or four different experiences of vulnerability is the best place to begin.

Most couples show considerable resistance to making these tapes, which may relate to anxiety about demonstrating incompetence. Most often, however, the taped exercises tap into some inevitable fears of getting too close, or of losing control of the distance from the partner.

Some pointers:

Select

1. A comfortable, private space.

2. A time when neither partner is tired, preoccupied, tense, or angry.

3. A time when interruptions will be absent or rare.

4. A recorder that produces clearly heard conversation.

The speaker should

1. Clarify that he or she wishes to be understood, not offered advice or judged.

2. Strive to tell the whole story of the experience rather than leaving out parts that are painful.

3. Strive to be very open about the feelings involved in the experience.

The listener should

1. Listen with a high level of attention.

2. Keep in mind that it is the partner's subjective reality, not the "truth," that is important.

3. Remember that the task is to facilitate the partner's exploration of the experience and not to direct the conversation.

4. Focus on the feelings expressed by the partner with no attempt to reassure or minimize those feelings.

5. Respond with reflections that indicate that the listener has heard and understands.

6. Use questions that open up rather than narrow the partner's story.

7. Avoid introducing new topics or changing the subject.

8. Avoid suggesting actions the partner might have taken or offering any solutions.

9. Avoid giving advice of any kind.

10. Avoid passing judgment on the partner's behavior.

After the initial conversations have been completed, it is helpful for both partners to listen to them together without making any comments. Each partner should listen, in particular, to how he or she responded to the partner's story. Only after this silent, reflective listening should the couple try to analyze the conversations.

In my clinical practice, the couple brings the tape to my office and the three of us analyze it together. I take the lead in this analytic process, but rely heavily on encouraging the couple to play a major role. After stopping the tape, I ask such questions as: "What do you hear yourself doing?" "How else might you have responded?" "Do you see how your question changes the topic?" "What do you hear in the tone of your voice?" "How could you have better acknowledged the fear he was experiencing?"

Some couples can do a good job of analyzing their own tapes; the foregoing outline provides a useful structure to follow in the analytic task. Convert each of the statements about the right situation, the speaker's task, and the more complicated job of the listener to a question. Either partner may ask the questions about the right situation. The listener should ask the speaker the questions based on the speaker's "dos" and "don'ts" and the speaker should ask those based on the listener's "dos" and "don'ts."

It is important to write down each mistake and keep the list. The list can then be reviewed before the exercise is repeated. The review might sound like this:

> "Jim, here's a list of your mistakes from our last exercise. You're supposed to read them out loud."
>
> "Well, okay. Last time I asked far too many focused questions.

I interrupted you a lot, and on several occasions, I told you how
you should have handled the situation."

This type of review alerts the listener to mistakes that he or
she should try to avoid in the next exercise. It is important,
however, for the couple to embark on the exercises with a clear
understanding that mistakes are the rule. I tell couples that exploratory conversations are, for many, a radical departure from
their customary way of conversing. It is helpful to emphasize
that repetition is crucial. Just as one cannot learn to play golf
or tennis without practice, one needs practice to learn a new
conversational structure. It is through many repetitions that this
new way of listening and talking with each other loses its aura
of artificiality and becomes more natural.

Some people continue to make the same mistakes over and
over again. They seem incapable of engaging in this way of
conversing despite their wanting very much to do so. In this
case, a mental health professional might be able to help them
to understand and overcome the learning blocks.

Most couples, however, can learn to be more effective with
this way of listening and responding. It then becomes important
that the couple set up several times a week for practice sessions, perhaps as part of an end-of-the-day review. One partner
describes an experience he or she had that day. The other responds by listening closely and responding empathically. The
speaker explores the experience, and then they switch roles.

Some couples come to recognize the major life themes that

pop up repeatedly in their accounts of different experiences. Although most of these themes involve disturbances in relationships with important others, some have more to do with the individual's relationship with himself or herself.

When you and your partner feel reasonably comfortable with your empathic skills, try moving to the much more difficult area of topics that involve disagreements, conflicts, or distressed feelings between the two of you. The process is exactly the same—the speaker strives to be clear, direct, and open about the problem issue and the painful feelings involved, while the listener attends closely, reflects empathically, and resists inclinations to argue, point out the "truth," minimize the speaker's discomfort, or change the direction of the conversation. *When both of you are able to share openly (without attacking) and respond empathically (without being defensive), you will have the skills to resolve problems in your relationship that previously were unsolvable.* This happens slowly, but I think you will be pleasantly surprised to see how much each bit of new learning will change the ambiance of your relationship. It does not take very long for these empathic moments to build toward fundamental and longlasting improvements in feelings of closeness and of being understood that will dramatically alter the amount of intimacy you will share.

chapter eight

Learning Separateness and Autonomy

There are two pathways to greater separateness and autonomy; through experiences in which one is alone and through those with an important other.

LEARNING ON ONE'S OWN

There has always been popular support for the idea that learning how to be more separate and autonomous must involve actual experiences in which one is encouraged or forced to function independently. Several personal experiences come to mind.

As part of our initiation into a college fraternity, my pledge class underwent an intense group experience involving much stress. The intent was to have us bond, to come together around something shared and stressful. After a number of such group experiences, we were exposed to a very different ordeal. Each of us was taken at night, alone and blindfolded, to a remote area, where we were left with no idea of where we were or how to return to familiar territory. This was supposed to accomplish two things: teach us self-sufficiency and demonstrate how much one needed the support and help of one's friends.

Another experience involved teaching little children to swim. At the time, there were two schools of thought on how to do this. One was to throw them into the deep end of the pool, only interrupting their frantic thrashing about if they seemed truly about to drown. The second method was to accompany them into the shallow end and do some hands-on teaching, gradually moving into deeper water. Both methods were meant to teach the kids how to swim independently.

Experiences that help one attain a stronger sense of a separate and autonomous self while alone share an important underlying process with developing the same characteristics in the context of an important relationship: they both involve conversation. When alone, one has conversations with one's self. Lost in the middle of the night, I asked myself a series of questions intended to clarify my dilemma. "Can I see any lights? Which way is the wind blowing? Do I want to go toward the north star or away from it?"

These conversations with one's self are designed to clarify; that is, to answer two bigger questions: "What do I know about what I am experiencing?" and "What can I do about it?" These are the same two issues that are paramount in such conversations with important others.

Thus, I believe that in circumstances of solitude, individuals have important conversations with themselves, the objective of which is to clarify what one thinks and what one should do. It is in that process of clarification that one comes to a deeper sense of who one is and how one differs from others. In this way, a stronger sense of a separate and autonomous self may develop.

DEVELOPING SEPARATENESS AND AUTONOMY WITHIN AN IMPORTANT RELATIONSHIP

There is no more moving account of a conversation with an important other that leads to a stronger sense of who one is than what Toni Morrison has Sixto say in her novel *Beloved*. When asked why in the world he walked each weekend to be with the Thirty Mile Woman, Sixto explains:

> "She is a friend of my mind. She gather me, that. The pieces I am, she gather them and give them back to me in all the right order. It's good, you know, when you got a woman who is a friend of your mind."

To use Morrison's evocative language, a person can come to know himself or herself better if he or she has a friend of the mind.

Three circumstances lend themselves to conversations that facilitate the growth of separateness and autonomy. One involves sharing uncertainty or confusion about an experience. The second comes out of conversations in which there is a clear difference of opinion between you and the important other. The third circumstance refers to those occasions when one partner provokes in the other a thought, feeling, or action that the other did not spontaneously have. These three circumstances create opportunities for the couple to engage in exploratory conversations aimed at clarifying the experience of one or both partners. Several communication processes will be helpful in all three.

- *Clear expression of feelings and thoughts is necessary.*

    Although there are occasions on which one is not sure of what one feels or thinks, it is almost always possible to talk about what one does know. "I'm not sure exactly what I feel" or "I'm struggling to sort out my thoughts" can inform the other of one's uncertainty and invite assistance in the process of clarifying. It is, of course, important when one is certain of one's thoughts or feelings to be as clear as possible with the important other. The use of "I" statements (such as "I think" or "I feel") is encouraged because hearing one's self make such declarations may help one feel more certain about who one is.

- *Encouraging further exploration of the thoughts and feelings is crucial.*

    At least some of the time, many feel the need to proceed cautiously, to test the listener's responsiveness before plunging in. In conversations with important others, we do this through indirection, tentativeness, and other signals that suggest that something needs to be talked about, but that its exact nature is yet to be identified. This cautious beginning tests the availability of the important other and his or her willingness to listen and interact.

    Another, more common reason why we don't always say exactly what is on our minds is that, in many situations, we really don't know exactly what is going on inside us until we talk about it, and receive help from an important other in exploring it. One often sorts out what is going on in one's mind by talking about it (or writing about it). From this perspective, words are not just the containers for our thoughts, but have a circular relationship. What we think influences what we say and what we say influences what we think.

    So, whether one is deliberately cautious at the beginning of a conversation or doesn't really know exactly what the inner experience is, what is essential is that the other respond in ways that encourage exploration. The essentials of exploratory conversations include:

1. Encouraging the other to keep talking about the experience without pushing the conversation in any particular

direction. This is done through empathic statements, general encouragers, or brief summaries.

2. Avoiding responses that shut down the exploration. These include topic changes, giving advice, looking or sounding uninterested or bored, and passing judgment.

3. Communicating interest in and respect for the other's subjective reality. Nothing is more important in conversations with important others than that each partner feel that his or her unique views, opinions, and feelings are understood and respected by the other.

SHARING UNCERTAINTY OR CONFUSION

The following conversations illustrate something of both the positive and negative approaches to helping one's partner explore an area of uncertainty.

Assume that a husband has joined his wife at the end of the working day. He is concerned about a conversation he had with his boss and describes the conversation to his wife.

"And so that's the deal. He gave me *no* encouragement about my future."

"Well, that is troubling. What do you make of it?"

"I'm not sure."

"I know you can't be sure, but what are your ideas?"

"Well, I hope that he was just preoccupied with other things. Maybe he wasn't *trying* to be discouraging."

"You've done so well for the company for such a long time."

"Yes. That's why I was worried and upset."

"Do you have any other thoughts about it?"

"No. I can't think of any real reason he would want to scare me."

"What have you thought to do about it?"

"I could forget it—or try to—but I think I may talk to him about it."

"Sounds like you're coming to the conclusion that it probably wasn't his intent to scare you, but that you need to check it out."

"Yes. It helps to talk it through."

The important issue here is that the husband used his wife to think through the likely meaning of his conversation with his boss and to plan his response. She helped him to clarify what he thought, and, in doing so, helped him define better who he was. A person's sense of his or her self as a separate and autonomous individual is developed and reinforced by such conversations with an important other, particularly if they take place when one is uncertain about what one thinks or should do.

Contrast that conversation with this very different one.

"And so that's the deal. He gave me *no* encouragement about my future."

"I've warned you time and time again that he's a rat. He is not to be trusted."

"Well, I'm not sure. It could be there were other things involved."

"Look, don't be naive. You've got to understand the way the world really is."

"What do you mean?"

"It's dog eat dog. All you've done for that company means nothing to that jerk."

"Well, I'm still pretty confused about the whole deal."

In this conversation, it is easy to see that a very different process was at work. The wife did not respond in ways that helped the husband to clarify what he thought; rather, she told him what to think. Regardless of whether or not she was right, her act of intrusiveness led to confusion rather than clarity for him. Although all of us may occasionally have such unfortunate conversations with important others, if they are more or less routine, they can interfere with our secure sense of who we are.

Thus, the first principle of learning separateness and autonomy is that we do so by expressing thoughts and feelings clearly, and that the responses of an important other may be crucial, particularly if they are strongly patterned. The first wife responded in ways that helped the husband arrive at a clearer definition of what *he* believed and what *he* should do. She encouraged his sense of a separate self and his capacity for autonomy. The second woman did neither. She told her husband what to think, and this resulted in his becoming *less* able to sort out for himself what he believed and what he should do. She missed an opportunity to encourage the development or reinforcement of his separateness and autonomy. Her responses to her husband were very powerful. To impose one's thoughts on another person, to insist that one's way of thinking about a situation is the "right" and "only" way, is very invasive. That is why, in watching marital and family videotapes, our research team members came to call it "mind rape." "What you *really* think . . ." and "Your *true* feelings are . . ." came to represent to us the invasion of one person by another. We also became very interested in how the invaded person responded. We saw examples of repulsed invasions even in young children. "Mommy, that's not what *I* think; maybe that's what *you* think," one seven-year-old responded, causing his mother to reconsider her attempted invasion.

So, power is involved in the transactions that, if strongly patterned, can influence an important other's sense of a separate and autonomous self. This leads to a second generalization about helping each other to develop a stronger sense of self: the greater the power differential between the two participants, the greater is the likelihood of invasion and failure to support the other's development of a secure identity as a separate and autonomous person.

Why should this be so? I believe that the way in which a power differential most likely operates is through lack of respect (or disrespect) for the partner's subjective reality. Two partners with relatively equal power are more apt to be respectful of each other's thoughts and feelings. A very dominant spouse, by contrast, is more likely to impose (or try to impose) his or her views on the less powerful spouse. It is an all-too-common irony that, when seen in couples therapy, such dominant spouses may complain about the partner's childlike behaviors ("She buys everything in sight," or "He is always late and irresponsible"), while invading that spouse's mind by telling him or her what to think and how to behave, thus interfering with the development of more adult levels of separateness and autonomy.

DISCUSSING A DIFFERENCE OF OPINION

Helping an important other to clarify what he or she is thinking when uncertain is, in many ways, easier than is the second set of relationship circumstances out of which may come an increased sense of a separate and autonomous self: those many occasions on which the two partners are in clear disagreement about a particular experience or decision. There are ways in which differences are customarily dealt with that either strengthen or impede the development of a separate, autonomous self.

Again, I will illustrate with two brief marital conversations. Assume that the wife has been offered a promotion involving greater responsibility, more travel, and an increase in salary. The promotion would be stressful, but also would take her to a new level in the company, a level that would open up future opportunities for senior management positions. It is clear from her conversation with her husband that he has many misgivings about her taking the promotion.

"So, if I hear you right, you're not sure I should take the promotion?"

"Well, I know it's complicated, but I'm *really* concerned about the demands it would make on you."

"And what else bothers you about it?"

"I'm trying to sort that out. Maybe it has something to do with us, with our relationship. Maybe I'm afraid our marriage will become less important to you."

"I had no idea that you had those feelings..."

"Well, I'm *not* really sure. There is *something* that makes me leery about the promotion. You'll be traveling a lot more. We'll be together less. And your boss said it would open more doors for you."

"Yes. And that's exciting for me. I sort of want to see how far I can go."

"What do you think that's all about?"

"I'm not sure."

"But you probably have got some sort of idea."

"I guess it's tied up with proving something to myself."

"Just to yourself?"

"It *could* have something to do with my dad. His attitudes about women—his not-too-subtle chauvinism."

"I wondered about that."

We don't know *what* this couple's decision will be, but this bit of conversation tells us something of *how* they approach an important difference of opinion. What is happening here is that each partner responds in ways that encourage the other to explore what he and she is experiencing. In this reciprocal exploration, both wife and husband are learning more about who they are. They do so through careful listening and responding in ways that respect each other's subjective reality and assist in the process of clarification.

There are, however, many ways in which the conversation can fail. Let's see how another couple might deal with the same difference of opinion.

"So, if I hear you right, you're not sure I should take the promotion?"

"I don't think it's a particularly good deal."

"What do you mean?"

"Well, for one thing, the money is not all that much."

"It's not bad. But more important, it opens up some more opportunities."

"He only said that. There is nothing sure about it."

"You know, it sounds to me like you've already made up your mind."

"I'm just trying to be realistic, trying to prevent you from making a mistake."

"But that's what I mean. You've made up your mind that it's a mistake. You never want to take any chances."

"And you are *always* ready to grab the first thing that comes along without thinking it through."

Here we see a very different process. There is no attempt by either partner to help the other explore the factors involved in their initial difference. Rather, they begin to escalate the disagreement by using provocative language, such as "you never" and "you are always." Although we also don't know where this conversation will end, the process suggests an expanding conflict in which neither partner may budge from his or her initial position and each may inflict pain on the other. What is very clear is that such a conversational process does not lead to increased self-knowledge for either. There is not much likelihood that either will end up with a clearer sense of who he or she is. A stronger sense of being valued as a separate and autonomous self does not result.

EXPERIENCING YOUR PARTNER'S FEELINGS AS YOUR OWN

The third circumstance, and perhaps the most difficult, arises when one partner ascribes to the other, or indirectly stimulates in the other, qualities that the other did not originally have. It raises the possibility of what mental health professionals call *projection* (or *projective identification*), the unconscious trading of personality qualities, motives, beliefs, and feelings.

The function of projection in marriage is seen as regulatory.

If one partner, for example, projects onto the other an unwanted feeling, the second partner may accept the projection, thereby assisting the other to deal with the feeling. At other times, however, the partner may refuse to accept the projection, and instead attempt to help the projecting partner better clarify the unwanted feeling. It is through "turned-down" projections and effective clarifications that partners help each other more completely understand who they are. Then, a better awareness of who one is can result in a stronger sense of separateness and autonomy.

Assume that a wife has informed her husband that their son's third-grade teacher has notified her that the boy's conduct in the classroom is unacceptable. Since he has exhibited no problematic behaviors elsewhere, she is uncertain—and, perhaps, doesn't believe—that the problem lies entirely with the son.

"I just don't think we're getting the whole story. There's something fishy about Mrs. Allen's conduct report. Josh is not a bad boy—if anything, he's shy and overly sensitive."

"I think you're right, and I'm getting angry. I want some proof of her accusations!"

"You really *do* sound angry."

"Well, why not? He's only a little boy, and she's a dried-up, old-maid school teacher!"

"You know, Dear, I feel better about the whole thing now that I see how involved with it you are."

In this brief conversation, it is possible that the wife's anxiety about the son's conduct report is projected onto her husband (he, also, probably has some of his own), who then expresses her anxiety through his anger. In doing so, he helps the wife regulate her anxiety, but at the cost of no further clarification of her understanding of the issues, and thus no strengthening of her own sense of self.

Contrast that interchange with a very different process, one that results in increased clarification.

> "I just don't think we're getting the whole story. There's something fishy about Mrs. Allen's conduct report. Josh is not a bad boy—if anything, he's shy and overly sensitive."
>
> "Yes. I wonder what it's all about. What are your ideas?"
>
> "Well, I want to think it's all her, but I'm sure she didn't give all her students a bad conduct report. So I'm left not knowing what role, if any, Josh may have played in it."
>
> "He's always been such a quiet little guy, more like you than me, perhaps..."
>
> "It's interesting that you say that. I was always such a scared, mousy little kid. And when my mother or a teacher said anything critical to me, it *really* hurt."
>
> "That may make you pretty sensitive to anything like that happening to Josh."

In this conversation, the husband does not accept and express the wife's anxiety, but responds in ways that encourage her to explore herself. She does so, and begins to get in touch with parts of herself that were stirred up by her son's conduct report. In this instance, the husband's responses led to clarification, particularly of the need to distinguish her own identity from that of her son. Such clarifications, growing out of turned-down projections, may lead to a stronger sense of a separate and autonomous self.

The Use of Confrontations

As pointed out previously, confrontations, if used correctly, can help an important other resolve contradictions in what he or she feels or thinks, and thus assist in the development of a clearer sense of self. However, confrontations are tricky in the sense that they can also disrupt communication and lead to anger and distance.

Confrontation is usually called for when the listener becomes aware of a contradiction in the other's description. The most common contradiction is between *what* is said and *how* it is said. To proclaim happiness with a sad voice or sadness with a smiling face is a clear contradiction. Something is being denied—usually the feeling with which one is struggling and may be trying to avoid facing.

Other contradictions involve statements of fact that appear to negate each other. Telling an important other that one wants to see a particular movie after giving a number of reasons why the movie is not supposed to be any good is an example of such a contradiction.

In teaching beginning therapists the process of confrontation, I emphasize that tentativeness is important. To say, "It
sounds as if..," is very different from "What you really mean
is . . ." The first statement calls the speaker's attention to the
contradiction, but does so in a way that gives the speaker the
opportunity to decide whether or not to explore the topic. It is,
therefore, respectful in two ways. First, it leaves the resolution
of the contradiction up to the speaker, and, second, it does not
impose the listener's solution on the speaker.

Confrontations that are both tentative and respectful aim to
assist the speaker in coming to a clearer understanding of an
inner conflict. As such, they can help an important other develop a better sense of what he or she is feeling or thinking,
and facilitate a stronger sense of personal identity.

An example of a confrontation that incorporates the principles noted above comes from a taped exercise of a couple near-
ing the end of therapy.

The husband had described an experience with his aging
father, who did not react to the news of the patient's promotion.

> "Well, that's it—he didn't say anything about it."
>
> "How disappointing."
>
> "Not particularly. It's just the way he is."
>
> "You're not upset?"
>
> "No." (Said with sadness)
>
> "Well, you kind of sound down."
>
> "I didn't know I sounded sad."
>
> "Kind of."

"Well, maybe I am. It's the same old story. Nothing ever pleases him."

"I know how that hurts—the same old story—all your life."

"I just have to face that I'm not going to get his approval and not let it hurt me."

"Maybe it is just one of those deals that has to hurt—at least some."

EXERCISES FOR COUPLES

At dinner, after seeing the movie *The English Patient*, my wife asked me what I thought it was about. I told her that I wasn't sure, but she persisted in her friendly inquiry. Her questions pushed me to clarify what I believed the major theme of the movie to be: the influence of the past on the present, and the questions of how one knows one's own past and that of important others, of how much the past is reconstructed out of present needs, and of whether important elements of the past can be undone or reversed. I told her that each of the four major characters seemed to be struggling with one or all of those issues.

Until my wife asked, I did not consciously know what I thought about the movie, and, over dinner, I also came to know something more about myself—my pleasure in analytic processes and my interest (personal, as well as professional) in the complex interface between the past and present.

1. *The important issue is that such conversations become a pattern.*

The topics are of minor consequence: they can refer to "big" things going on in the world or "little" things, such as one's reaction to a movie. To start with, however, it is often wise to select topics that do not involve the marital relationship itself. Use more neutral topics. The listener should begin with broad, open-ended questions: "What do you think?" "What's your reaction to that?" "How do you put all of that together?" These questions are designed to invite the other to begin exploring his or her reactions to, or interpretations of, a particular report or theme.

2. *As in all exploratory conversations, the facilitator sticks closely to the other's material and tries not to interject his or her interpretations or theories.*

The facilitator also avoids responses that shut down the other's exploration, such as changing the topic, giving advice, being critical, or acting as if uninterested. The goal is to help the other *clarify what he or she believes or feels* about the topic.

3. *Empathic responses are the most important technique for promoting a sense of connection and intimacy.*

It is, however, important to understand that empathic responses also lead to further exploration, and thus to the possibility of a stronger sense of how one is different. Empathy is the direct route to intimacy, but, to the extent that it facilitates self-exploration, it can also be the road to a greater realization of differences, and hence a stronger sense of one's separateness.

4. *In all the exercises, respect for your partner's subjective reality is a central process.*

One must be able to put aside one's own agenda (at least temporarily) and focus all of one's attention on what is going on inside of one's partner.

5. *Clarifications and confrontations are the essential processes in helping an important other become more aware of who he or she is.*

6. *After some practice with more neutral topics, many couples can move on to exploring each other's subjective reality about their relationship.*

Here, again, the temptation is strong to debate, respond defensively, or in some other way move the focus away from the clarification of each other's subjective reality.

The following outline may help to organize your efforts.

- Select a neutral topic.
- Ask your partner to share his or her personal responses to the topic.
- Use exploratory conversational techniques to encourage as much discussion of the topic by your partner as seems possible.
- Keep uppermost in mind that the only objective is clarification of the other's position.
- After making this kind of conversational process more or less routine through many repetitions, you can turn to the more charged area of the relationship itself.
- Select relationship topics that your partner either seems uncertain about or on which he or she clearly has a different opinion from your own.
- Keep in mind that the goal is to clarify what one's partner believes.
- Reverse the roles of the explorer and the facilitator so that growth can be true of both partners.

Finally, to develop a stronger sense of one's self as a separate and autonomous person, I return to Morrison's lovely phrase: Everyone needs at least one *friend of the mind*. To have such a "friend" can mean both a stronger sense of connection and a stronger sense of separateness. In the best of all circumstances, partners are *friends of the mind* for each other.

—✑—

chapter nine

Afterthoughts

Many couples are systematic in their approach to certain issues. You get a physical examination every few years, change the oil in your car every six months or so, and have your home heating system checked out every fall. You balance your checkbook every month or so, and keep records of your income tax payments.

But, regardless of how systematic you may be, it is unlikely that you and your spouse ever take the time to do a marital checkup. Despite the fact that there is no more important influence on the quality of life than the nature of one's central relationship, we do not do inventories of marital assets and liabilities.

Sitting down with your spouse and asking each other a few questions can get the process started.

Which type of marriage (Chapter 6) seems to characterize us best?

What would each of us like to change about our relationship?

Do we need to learn how to have a closer relationship?

Do we need to work on each of us being more independent?

How can we have more fun together?

What is it that I can do to make the relationship better for you?

This book is an effort to bring that which I have learned from my personal life, clinical work, and research to the attention of readers who want more from their marriages.

INTERPERSONAL RELATIONSHIPS ARE FOR BETTER OR WORSE

The popular press is replete with reports of scientific research suggesting that the infant's relationships with significant others influence how his or her brain develops. I do not believe that relationships affect brain function only in infancy, but that their impact is felt throughout life. The brain systems both for connecting with others and for functioning independently continue to need relationships in which both connecting and functioning alone are experienced in order to stay alive. If you don't use your brain systems, they atrophy. So the "for better or worse" metaphor applies not only to satisfaction, emotional health, and life's meaning, but also to the ongoing changes in the structure of our brains.

You Have a Great Deal to Say About What Goes On in Your Central Relationships

We have no control over who our parents are, what went on in their relationship, and whether we were neglected, or abused, or loved. The same neglect or abuse need not characterize our adult relationships, however. Here we do have something to say. Couples therapists believe that how a couple's relationship plays out is almost always a shared responsibility (except possibly in such cases as those involving physical violence, which must be understood as an individual responsibility). I realize that some people are firmly fixed in their views that they are pure victims of their partners' personalities or malevolence. To the extent that the victim identity is held onto, one is powerless. But when one understands that relationships are always constructed by two people, one has the power either to try to change the relationship or to terminate it.

Relationships Can Heal

Although we still have much to learn about it, marital healing is a reality. Many people do work through harmful childhood experiences with an adult partner. They are transformed by love. There are many roads to achieving healing. From my understanding of successful relationships (marital, parent–infant, and psychotherapeutic), several processes emerge as vitally important: (1) the establishment of a strong feeling bond, (2) the capability to repair the inevitable breaks in that bond, and (3) the ability to become a more independent, self-sufficient person.

It is, then, the relationships that encourage both strong bonding and individual autonomy that are most likely to be healing.

These are the fundamental insights. There remains, however, something to say about process.

Constructing and Maintaining a Healing Process Is Hard Work

There is no simple method that does all the work; nothing but sustained effort has a chance. You can change your relationship with your self through individual therapy, and that may change your relationship with your partner for better or worse. To change a relationship directly, however, usually requires the participation of both partners. So, it is hard work and joint effort that are required.

IMPROVING A RELATIONSHIP GOES FORWARD AND BACKWARD

The old adage of two steps forward and one step back applies to the process of changing a relationship. Remember that the basic structure of your relationship may have been in place for years. Giving up old patterns—regardless of how self-defeating and uncomfortable they may be—is never easy. New patterns must be used over and over again before they replace the old, entrenched ones. Slipping back to the old ways is inevitable, but must not impair the effort. You can learn something each time you and your partner revert to the old patterns.

THE MOST POWERFUL WAY TO CHANGE A RELATIONSHIP IS BY CHANGING HOW YOU TALK WITH EACH OTHER

How partners treat each other—the physical aspects of their relationship—is often their way of communicating. For these partners, the avoidance of physical contact and intimidating and other behaviors are their primary ways of sending messages to each other—messages that would be more clearly communicated with words.

It is often said that language is the highest achievement of the human species. To use language, and use it well, is crucial in establishing enduring relationships. In particular, language is a major way of either getting closer to another person or keeping your distance. My couples therapy relies heavily on helping couples to learn the effective use of conversation in establishing both intimacy and autonomy. To change a marriage, the partners will find that they have to talk, probably more than they have ever talked before.

Expressions of gratitude and remorse are essential in the healing process. In many ways, this is the simplest task involved in changing a relationship. The ability to say, "Thank you for telling me about that," and "I'm sorry I didn't listen well enough when you needed me to," is a powerful tool both in establishing a strong feeling bond and, when necessary, in repairing that bond. Too often, we forget how helpful such words can be.

Finally, I wish to address a question I am asked from time to time: "Aren't you just teaching couples to be better actors? To say things that they may not truly feel? To accept a partner's subjective reality when one really feels it is way out of line?" My answer is this: "Just as feelings and thoughts influence what we say, what we say influences what we feel and think. The relationship is circular." So, I start with the mechanics of communication. Teaching people to talk with each other in ways that are associated with intimacy and autonomy usually leads to their feeling more intimate and being more autonomous.

I hope that you will share this approach with your partner and experiment with my suggestions. Remember, there is no more powerful determinant of how well your life can be lived than the quality of your relationships with those with whom you spend that life.

Suggested Readings

Ainsworth, M.D.S. (1989): Attachments beyond infancy. *Am Psychol* 44:709–716.

Beavers, W.R. (1985): *Successful Marriage: A Family Systems Approach to Couples Therapy.* New York: Norton.

Bowlby, J. (1983): *Attachment and Loss. Vol. 1: Attachment* (2nd ed.). New York: Basic Books.

Bowlby, J. (1976): *Attachment and Loss. Vol. 2: Separation: Anxiety and Anger.* New York: Basic Books.

Bowlby, J. (1982): *Attachment and Loss. Vol. 3: Loss: Sadness and Depression.* New York: Basic Books.

Cohn, D.A. Silver, D.H., Cowan, C.P., Cowan, P.A., and Pearson, J. (1992): Working models of childhood attachment and couple relationships. *J Family Issues* 13:432–449.

Gottman, J. (1994): *Why Marriages Succeed or Fail* (with N. Silver). New York: Simon & Schuster.

Hendrix, H. (1990): *Getting the Love You Want: A Guide for Couples.* New York: Harper & Row.

Hendrix, H. (1992): *Keeping the Love You Find: A Guide for Singles.* New York: Pocket Books.

Horvath, A.O., and Luborsky, L. (1993): The role of the therapeutic alliance in psychotherapy. *J Consult Clin Psychol* 61:561–573.

Johnson, S.J., and Greenberg, L.S. (Eds.) (1994): *The Heart of the Matter: Perspectives of Emotion in Marital Therapy.* New York: Brunner/Mazel.

Kramer, P.D. (1989): *Moments of Engagement: Intimate Psychotherapy in a Technological Age.* New York: Norton.

Kramer, P.D. (1993): *Listening to Prozac.* New York: Penguin Books.

Lewis, J.M. (1978): *To Be a Therapist: The Teaching and Learning.* New York: Brunner/Mazel.

Lewis, J.M. (1979): *How's Your Family?* New York: Brunner/Mazel.

Lewis, J.M. (1986): Family structure and stress. *Fam Process* 25:235–247.

Lewis, J.M. (1988): The transition to parenthood. I: The rating of prenatal marital competence. *Fam Process* 27:149–165.

Lewis, J.M. (1988): The transition to parenthood. II: Stability and change in marital structure. *Fam Process* 17:273–283.

Lewis, J.M. (1989): *The Birth of the Family: An Empirical Inquiry.* New York: Brunner/Mazel.

Lewis, J.M. (1991): *Swimming Upstream: Teaching Psychotherapy in a Biological Era.* New York: Brunner/Mazel .

Lewis, J.M. (1991): Thirty years of teaching psychotherapy skills. *Int J Group Psychother* 41:419–432.

Lewis, J.M. (1997): *Marriage as a Search for Healing: Theory, Assessment, and Therapy.* New York: Brunner/Mazel.

Lewis, J.M. (1998): For better or worse: Interpersonal relationships and individual outcome. *Am J Psychiatry* 155:582–589.

Lewis, J.M., Beavers, W.R., Gossett, J.T., and Phillips, V.A. (1976): *No Single Thread: Psychological Health in Family Systems.* New York: Brunner/Mazel.

Lewis, J.M., and Looney, J.G. (1983): *The Long Struggle: Well-Functioning Working-Class Black Families.* New York: Brunner/Mazel.

Luborsky, L. (1977): Measuring a pervasive psychic structure in psychotherapy: The core conflictual relationship theme. In N. Freedman and S. Grand (Eds.), *Communicative Structures and Psychic Structures.* New York: Plenum.

Morrison, T. (1988): *Beloved.* New York: Plume Printing.

Shields, C. (1995): *The Stone Diaries.* New York: Penguin Books.

Valliant, G.E. (1977): *Adaptation to Life.* Boston: Little, Brown.

190   •   *Suggested Readings*

Waring, E.M. (1988): *Enhancing Marital Intimacy Through Facilitating Cognitive Self-disclosure.* New York: Brunner/Mazel.

Weingarten, K. (1991): The discourses of intimacy: Adding a social constructionist and feminist view. *Fam Process* 30:285–305.

Weingarten, K. (1992): A consideration of intimate and non-intimate interactions in therapy. *Fam Process* 31:45–59.

Young, J.E. (1994): *Cognitive Therapy for Personality Disorders: A Schema-Focused Approach.* Sarasota, Fla.: Professional Resource Press.

Appendix

TIMBERLAWN COUPLE AND FAMILY EVALUATION SCALES*
Jerry M. Lewis, M.D.
John T. Gossett, Ph.D.
Margaret Tresch Owen, Ph.D.
M. Matthew Housson, Ph.D.[†]

*From Lewis, J. M., Gossett, J. T., Owen, M. T., & Housson, M. M. (1997). *Timberlawn Couple and Family Evaluation Scales*. Dallas, TX: Timberlawn Psychiatric Research Foundation, Inc.

[†] Staff members, trainees, and volunteers who participated in the development of these scales in addition to the authors include:

Bill Barfoot	Sara J. Henry, M.S.	Ann S. Supina
F. David Barnhart, M.A.	Cheryl Kennedy, M.Ed.	David A. Tinney
Beth Bontempo, Ph.D.	Mary Anne Leistra	Maureen Tlapek-Koshakji,
Nanette L. Bruchey	Julie Ann Mason, Ph.D.	M.S.
Melissa Anne Cahill, Ph.D.	Norma M. Muldoon	Angela B. Vaughn
Maureen P. Crowley, M.A.	Beverly A. Mulvihill, Ph.D.	Anne M. Ware, Ph.D.
David G. Fyffe	Carol Norris, M.S.	Sue Ashe Wetsel, M.S.W.
Margaret R. Geiger	Virginia Austin Phillips	Ellen C. Wheatley, Ph.D.
Patricia Pater Green	Jane Schwarz, R.N.	Philip J. White
	Kathy Shores-Wilson, Ph.D.	

CONTENTS

TIMBERLAWN COUPLE AND FAMILY EVALUATION SCALES

Instructions: The following scales are designed to assess family or couple functioning on continua representing interactional aspects of being a family or a couple. It is important that you consider the entire range of each scale when you make your ratings. Please try to respond on the basis of what you see and hear rather than what you imagine might occur elsewhere. *Please circle the numbers on the scales that reflect your assessments.*

I. STRUCTURE

    A. *Overt Power:* The manner in which interpersonal influence is distributed within the couple or family.

        1. *Chaotic or Alienated:* Fragmented or disorganized; no one structures the interaction; tasks rarely if ever get accomplished; or, markedly disruptive behavior is ignored or dealt with ineffectually; or, each participant pursues a different agenda; topic of conversation changes frequently so that the discussion approaches incoherence; or, participants are disengaged or alienated from one another; no one is able to facilitate engagement.

        2. *Conflicted:* Participants seek control and compete for power. The struggle may be subtle (with reciprocal topic changes, interrogations, and interruptions) or gross (with conflicting directives, mutual blaming, and verbal attacks). No one participant can establish dominance.

        3. *Dominated with Conflict:* One participant clearly possesses the most overt power, but one or more others seek control and compete for power. There is little or no sharing and no true negotiation.

        4. *Dominated with Complementarity:* One participant clearly possesses the most overt power, and others rarely if ever seek control or compete for power. There may be some sharing of power and some ne-

gotiation; the dominant person sometimes is open to information (influence) from other family members.

5. *Led or Shared:* Power is shared among the participants, respecting the age and competence of each. Different individuals may be "in charge" for different tasks as various skills are used to accomplish goals.

B. *Adult Leadership:* (To be scored only when two or more generations are present.)

Adult leadership involves providing direction in the context of respect. Respect includes consideration of others' beliefs and feelings and an openness to their value, but does not require agreement. Direction includes guidance, instruction, and firmness appropriate to the context. Adult leadership is assessed by the degree to which the adult(s) provide the child(ren) with age-appropriate levels of both dimensions, independent of the proportion of leadership provided by each parent.

1. *Poor:* Little or no adult leadership.

2.

3. *Fair:* The adult(s) attempt to provide leadership, but the effort is either intermittent or relinquished.

4.

5. *Good:* The adult(s) provide high levels of leadership.

C. *Inappropriate Parent-Child Coalition:* (To be scored only when two or more generations are present.)

An intense parent-child coalition in which the participants exclude and may collude against other family members. This "special" relationship may be one of over-involvement, or it may be angry, argumentative, eroticized, or competitive.

Behavioral markers might include: nonverbal signals that appear to exclude others (e.g., smiles, sighs, glances); verbal exchanges that appear age-inappropriate; inappropriate or excessive physical contact between parent and child.

1. *Clear evidence* of an inappropriate parent-child relationship.

2.

3. *Some evidence* of an inappropriate parent-child relationship.

4.

5. *No evidence* of an inappropriate parent-child relationship.

D. *Closeness:* The degree to which family members share perceptions, interests, beliefs, activities, friends, values, and pleasurable time together.

1. *Little evidence of closeness.*

2.

3. *Somewhat close.*

4.

5. *Very close.*

II. AUTONOMY

A. *Clarity of Expression:* The degree to which family members clearly express individual values, opinions, or ideas. (Do not rate clarity of expression of *feelings* on this scale.)

Behavioral markers might include: speech that is clear, not mumbled or inaudible; the absence of obscure language; the ability to voice irritation/frustration verbally instead of through nonverbal behaviors; the ability to make "I" statements (e.g., "I think," "I believe").

1. *Indistinct:* Family members generally are obscure.

2.

3. *Somewhat vague:* Some members are quite clear while others are obscure; or, members sometimes are clear and sometimes are not.

4.

5. *Distinct:* Family members generally articulate individual expressions clearly.

B. *Respect for Subjective Reality:* The extent to which family members respond to each other with clear regard for the other's views. A crucial test occurs when the respondent disagrees but does not challenge the right of the other to have such views.

Behavioral markers might include: careful listening, frequent acknowledgments, and requests for clarifications; attentiveness; turning toward the speaker, making eye contact, expressing patience, or not changing the subject.

1. *Members show little if any respect* by not listening or responding or by labeling others' views as untrue, unthinkable, ludicrous, contemptible, or crazy.

2.

3. *Some members show respect* for the views of others and some do not, or most members sometimes do and sometimes do not show respect for others' views.

4.

5. *Members most often react to others' views by respectfully listening*, acknowledging, and responding, whether or not they agree.

C. *Responsibility:* The degree to which family members accept accountability for their beliefs and feelings and their past, present, and future actions.

Behavioral markers might include: the ability to make statements that claim responsibility (e.g., "Yes, I was wrong," "I made a mistake"); the ability to admit to guilt and acknowledge imperfections; the absence of blaming statements.

1. *Members rarely*, if ever, accept responsibility for their beliefs, feelings, or actions. Typically others are blamed, excuses are made, their own beliefs, feelings, or actions are denied, or the members' behaviors contradict their words.

2.

3. *Members sometimes* accept responsibility for their beliefs, feelings, or actions, but tactics sometimes include blaming others, speaking in 3rd person, using plural pronouns, or demonstrating behaviors that contradict their words.

4.

5. *Members almost always* accept responsibility for their own beliefs, feelings, and actions.

III. PROBLEM SOLVING

A. *Closure:* The ability to reach a solution during the time provided.

1. *Poor:* No closure achieved either because there appears to be little or no real involvement with the problem or no decision among possible solutions.

2.

3. *Fair:* Partial closure is achieved, but participants do not deal with all of the obvious aspects of the problem.

4.

5. *Good:* Complete closure is achieved on all obvious aspects of the problem.

B. *Use of Negotiation:* The degree to which family members accept individual differences and work together for consensus or for resolution of differences through agreement or compromise.

Behavioral markers might include: the participation of all members so that everyone has a "voice" in the process; the ability to recognize differences and ask for and/or be open to input from all members; the ability to respect differences of opinion; the ability to search for compromises when there is disagreement.

1. *No evidence* of negotiation.

2.

3. *Some negotiation* occurs, but family members do not always listen to different members' perspectives or do not always strive to reach consensus or compromise; or, one or more members do not participate.

4.

5. *Members demonstrate* acceptance of individual differences, work together to resolve those differences, search for consensus, and show the capacity for compromise.

IV. AFFECT REGULATION

A. *Expressiveness:* The openness with which affects are expressed.

1. *Closed down:* The interaction appears to be closed down affectively. There is little, if any, open expression of affect.

2. *Guarded:* The interaction is affectively guarded. Few affects are expressed openly. Affect is primarily expressed through subtle facial expressions, postures, or other nonverbal mechanisms.

3. *Selective:* Some affects are expressed openly but others are not, or affect is expressed openly by some participants but not others.

4. *Mostly open:* Affects are openly expressed by most of the participants with only occasional restriction or avoidance of affective expression.

5. *Open:* Affects are openly expressed by all participants.

B. *Responsiveness:* The more-or-less characteristic way in which participants respond to affects expressed by family members.

1. *Punished:* Affects are responded to with critical, condescending, or punitive messages.

2. *Avoided:* Affects are often not responded to, or the response is avoidant in the sense that it addresses only the content, suggests action, or changes the subject.

3. *Inconsistent:* Affects are responded to inconsistently. Some participants acknowledge affects and others do not, or some affects are acknowledged and others are not.

4. *Cognitive empathy:* Affects are often acknowledged by participants. The acknowledgment does not appear to involve affective arousal in the respondents.

5. *Affective empathy:* Affects are often acknowledged by participants, and the acknowledgment appears to involve affective arousal such that there is a shared affective state.

C. *Positive Regard:* Members express warmth toward, pleasure with, acceptance of, and affection for one another. Positive regard may be shown verbally or nonverbally.

Ratings are based on both the strength and quantity of positive regard expressed.

Behavioral markers might include: praise and expressions of enjoyment of one another, or speaking in a warm tone of voice to each other; smiling and laughing together, a relaxed and comfortable presence together, and displays of affection.

1. *Members show little or no positive regard* for each other.

2.

3. *Positive regard is shown* with moderate frequency and strength, or positive regard is shown for some members but not others.

4.

5. *Members express positive regard strongly* and frequently for each other.

D. *Negative Regard:* Members refuse to participate with one another or engage in disrespectful conversations or activities that interfere with task completion. Ratings are based on both the strength and quantity of negative regard expressed.

Behavioral markers might include: criticism, disapproval or sarcasm; contemptuous, hostile or threatening words or actions; tense body and facial muscles; angry, harsh, or irritated vocal tones directed to other members, or sullen silence or pouting.

1. *Members express negative regard strongly* and frequently for each other.

2.

3. *Negative regard is shown* with moderate frequency and strength, or negative regard is shown for some members but not others.

4.

5. *Members show little or no negative regard* for each other.

E. *Mood and Tone:* The overall feeling or affective tone of the interaction, based on the frequency of affective expression.

1. *Usually negative* (cold, distancing, angry, hateful, hopeless, pessimistic, cynical, suspicious, contemptuous).

2.

3. *Flat affect predominates,* or a mixture of negative and positive affective tone.

4.

5. *Usually positive* (warm, affiliative, admiring, loving, hopeful, optimistic, accepting, trusting, humorous).

F. *Empathy:* The degree to which individuals are sensitive to each other's feelings and communicate verbally or nonverbally their understanding of those feelings. At deeper levels, empathy involves actually experiencing that which another person is feeling.

Behavioral markers might include: nonverbal signs of experiencing that which has been expressed by the speaker (e.g., sighs, moans, tears); verbal signs of knowing the other person's experience (e.g., "I know what it's like to be angry like that," "No wonder you felt_____," "It must be frustrating for you").

1. *Feelings are discounted,* or not responded to; there is no empathic responsiveness.

2.

3. *There is some suggestion* of a capacity for empathic responsiveness, but it is not clearly evident.

4.

5. *Empathic responsiveness* is clearly evident.

V. DISAGREEMENT/CONFLICT

Disagreement is an affectively neutral difference of opinion, belief, idea, or feeling. *Conflict* involves active opposition with a sense of struggle, strife, antagonism, fighting, or ill will.

A. *Frequency*

   1. *Much or all of the interactions* are characterized by conflict.

   2.

   3. *One or a small number of conflicts* occur during the observed interactions.

   4.

   5. *There may or may not be disagreements,* but there are no conflicts.

B. *Affective Quality:* Conflicts may be addressed with respect for the other person(s) or with a variety of negative affects and behaviors.

Behavioral markers of disrespect include: disparagement, dismissal, rejection, whining, complaining, criticism, sarcasm, inattention, coercion, moralistic disapproval, direct attack, character assassination, or contempt. Also included may be an icy, distant, or superior style or a mocking or belittling tone.

   1. *One or more conflicts are addressed with clear* and intense forms of negative affects or behaviors noted above.

2.

3. *One or more conflicts are addressed with mild* forms of negative affects or behaviors noted above.

4.

5. *Conflicts do not occur,* or if they occur, are handled with respect.

C. *Generalization and Escalation:* One or more participants expand the content of disagreements or conflicts beyond the original focus or intensify the original affect in a negative direction. In extreme cases this involves attacks on the personality, character, or worth of the other.

Behavioral markers might include: statements that allude to past instances of conflict (e.g., "That reminds me of all the other times _____;") frequent use of "you always . . . ," or, "you never . . . ;" a sense of lack of resolution of conflict.

1. *Disagreements or conflicts characteristically* are generalized and/or escalated.

2.

3. *Some escalation or generalization occurs,* but one or more participants act to contain the escalation or generalization.

4.

5. *Disagreements or conflicts do not occur,* or if they occur, are engaged without escalation or generalization to additional topics.

VI. GLOBAL COMPETENCE

Global competence is defined as the extent to which a couple or family system has characteristics that encourage the development of both separateness and connectedness in its members.

Please circle the number that most closely approximates the characteristics observed in the couple or family to be rated.

1. The couple or family is *chaotic or alienated*; there is no adult leadership, and inappropriate parent-child relationships may be present. Often there appears to be a kind of closeness in which individual boundaries are blurred, or, the participants seem totally disengaged or alienated from one another. Individuals are often unclear about beliefs, fail to respect the subjective realities of others, and may avoid responsibility for their thoughts, beliefs, and actions. Problem-solving is characterized by a lack of closure and an absence of negotiation. Affects are often closed down or guarded. Responsiveness to affect is avoided or punished. It is often difficult to assess the levels of positive and negative regard. The prevailing mood is either negative or flat, empathy is absent or rare. Disagreement and conflict are not predominant characteristics, but if they occur, they may involve contempt. Generalization and escalation may be seen but are not typical.

2.

3. The couple or family is *disorganized by intense conflict* which is severe enough to make problem-solving difficult or impossible. Many of the exchanges involve personal attacks. Contempt is often noted.

Generalizations and escalations are commonplace. The intensity of the disorganizing conflict frequently precludes adult leadership. There may be relatively stable or transient inappropriate parent-child coalitions as the children are drawn into or enter the conflict. Closeness is not present. Although each participant's individual statements may be clear and understandable, there is little or no respect shown for the opinions of others, and negotiation is absent. Responsibility is often avoided; externalizations and projections are common as the warring individuals often ascribe malignant motivations to each other. Although anger dominates the interaction, other affects are most often absent. Expressions of affect often are punished or avoided. In particular, positive regard is rare and empathy is not seen.

4.

5.   The couple or family is characterized by the presence of *conflict which may be of moderate or severe intensity but does not lead to disorganization.* Adult leadership is compromised and inappropriate parent-child coalitions are frequent. Closeness is rare or absent. Participants are clear in most of their expressions, but there is little respect for each other's subjective reality and little or no acceptance of responsibility for one's behaviors. Although problem-solving can occur, it is most often compromised by the tendency for generalization and escalation of the conflict, and negotiation is rare or absent. The expression of affects other than anger and its derivatives is limited and responses to each other are of a very low order. Negative regard prevails; positive regard is absent. The overall tone of the interaction is angry; empathy is absent, while contempt is often observed.

6.

7.   The couple or family is characterized by *subdued or muted conflict which may be present all the time or appear suddenly, often in*

the absence of clear precipitants. The participants appear to be civilized in their battle for control; it is as if they had learned well the rules of parlor conflict. They rarely attack each other in frontal fashion, rather it is through innuendo, expressions of disdain, and icy reserve. Generalizations are sometimes seen, but intense escalation is rare. Leadership is compromised, and children may be triangled into the conflict. Closeness is either absent or appears in a modest way between episodes of conflict. The participants are clear in their expressions but show limited capacity for responsibility or respect for the subjective realities of others. Although negotiation is rare, problems can be approached and solutions reached despite the hostile jabs and counterattacks. The participants express anger, but other affects, particularly those associated with caring, are rarely seen. Responses to the expressions of affect are inconsistent or blunted, but are often couched in politeness. Negative regard predominates; positive regard is rare. The mood is mostly cool, and empathy is absent.

8.

9. The couple or family is characterized by a *dominant member who appears to be in complete or near complete control of the interaction. Although one or more other participants may express resentment indirectly* through facial expression, body movements, or other channels, direct confrontations are relatively rare. Problem-solving most often involves only the dominant member. Parent-child alliances that appear oppositional to the dominant member are sometimes seen. True negotiation is not seen. Closeness is rare. Participants are usually clear in expressing their thoughts. Respect for subjective reality may be present in some participants, but is absent in the dominant member. Avoidance of responsibility is often noted. Feelings are often expressed indirectly, and open responsiveness is

seen only at times. Positive regard is often absent or present in low levels. Negative regard is apparent through sullenness and indirect expressions. The overall mood is negative, and empathy is rare. Open conflict is seldom seen; there is little respect and the dominant member may express contempt for others. He or she may generalize negative attributions, but escalations are not usually seen.

10.

11. The couple or family is characterized by the *presence of a moderately dominant member whose authority and control seem generally acceptable to other participants.* If conflict or resentment is noted, it is usually of brief duration and remains relatively circumscribed. Closeness may be present, often in the form of respect. There are usually no inappropriate parent-child coalitions. Thoughts and opinions are usually clearly expressed and most often responded to directly. Respect for subjective reality may be noted on some occasions and not others. Problem-solving usually involves partial closure, but negotiation is not typical. Feelings are sometimes openly expressed and on other occasions are muted. Participants most often acknowledge each other's feelings. There are often moderate levels of both positive and negative regard. The overall mood is often more polite than warm and affectionate. Empathy is sometimes seen. Conflict is usually absent, respect is common, and generalizations rare. Escalations are the exception.

12.

13. The couple or family is characterized by *a pattern of subtle dominance or, in some instances, of shared power.* One or both adults can provide leadership to the system and little conflict is apparent. There is a good deal of respect within the system and little evidence

of generalization or escalation. Closeness seems somewhat restricted, but there is little evidence of inappropriate parent-child coalitions. The participants communicate clearly, often take responsibility for their individual thoughts and behaviors, and demonstrate a moderate capacity to respect each other's subjective reality. Problems may be handled with partial to complete closure, and some negotiation may be observed. In the affective realm, however, these couples or families demonstrate a constricted range of expressiveness, only moderate levels of responsiveness, and an obvious lack of spontaneity. Although they seem to like each other, clear and frequent expressions of affection are rare. Negative regard, if seen, is likely to be mild. The mood is formal and polite. Empathy is limited.

14.

15.   The couple or family is characterized by *one adult taking a clear leadership role in which he or she is respectful of the thoughts and feelings of other participants.* It is clear that he or she is the captain of the team, and there is little, if any, evidence of opposition to this leadership. He or she solicits opinions from other participants, but in the absence of consensus or easy compromise clearly reserves the right to have the final say. There is no evidence of inappropriate parent-child coalitions. The participants appear to feel close to each other, and they usually achieve complete closure on problem issues, often relying on negotiation. Thoughts are expressed clearly and others respond appropriately. There is evidence of considerable respect for each other's subjective reality. Individuals take responsibility for their thoughts, opinions, and behaviors. A wide range of affects are expressed without apparent fear of consequences. Positive regard predominates, and there is little evidence of negative affects. Empathy is seen, and the overall mood is warm and caring. Although disa-

greements occur, conflict is infrequent, and when present does not involve contempt, generalization, or escalation.

16.

17.   The couple or family is characterized by *shared leadership*. There is obvious closeness and no inappropriate parent-child coalitions. Participants are clear in their expressions, responsible for their thoughts and behaviors, and demonstrate high levels of respect for each other's subjective realities. Problem-solving is characterized by complete closure and negotiation is common. A wide range of affects are freely expressed and responded to in ways that are affirming. Positive regard dominates the interaction; negative regard is rarely observed. Empathy is often noted, and the overall mood is one of caring and affection. Although disagreements can be noted, conflicts are rare and, when seen, are not characterized by generalization or escalation, but rather are handled with respect.

Index

A

Abandonment, 81, 124
  fear of, 30, 54, 120
Achiever role, 90
Adolescence, 8, 9
Adult leadership, 194
Affect regulation, 200–204
Alienated marriage, 127–130
Aloneness, 37, 47
Altered memories, 77–78
Ambivalent attachment, 49–50
Anger, 18–20, 90, 124, 150,
  151
Anxiety, 21, 28, 55, 63
Approval seeking, 83
Assertiveness, 14, 25
Autonomy, 4, 10–11, 30, 47,
  61, 112, 123, 186, 196–198
  learning, 159–179
  as part of separateness, 43
Avoidance, as self-protective
  style, 82
Avoidant attachment, 49

B

Bad child role, 89–90
Bad seed role, 91–92
Belief system, 95
Beloved (Morrison), 161
Blandness, 90
Blood pressure, 32, 124
Brain systems, 48, 73, 134, 182–
  183

C

Caretaker role, 90, 91, 93
Caretaking, as self-protective
  style, 82
Casual conversations, 137
Central problematic
  relationships, memories of,
  80–87, 93–94
Change, ability to deal with,
  110–113
Chaotic pattern of power
  distribution, 65, 68–69